Performance Appraisal for Sport and Recreation Managers

Joanne MacLean, PhD
University of Windsor

Human Kinetics

Library of Congress Cataloging-in-Publication Data

MacLean, Joanne, 1959-
   Performance appraisal for sport and recreation managers / Joanne MacLean.
     p. cm.
   Includes bibliographical references (p.) and index.
   ISBN 0-7360-3642-3
    1. Sports personnel--Rating of. 2. Sports administration--Evaluation. 3.
   Sports--Management--Evaluation. I. Title.
   GV713 .M335 2001
   796'.06'93--dc21

                                             2001024451

ISBN: 0-7360-3642-3

The bulleted list on pages 107-108 is adapted from THE COMPLETE GUIDE TO PERFORMANCE APPRAISALS. Copyright © 1996 Richard Charles Grote. Adapted by permission of the publisher, AMACOM, a division of American Management Association International, New York, NY. All rights reserved. http://www.amacombooks.org

Appendix A.7 is adapted from Sport Canada, 1987, Human resource management and national coaches (Canada, Ottawa: Ministry of Supply and Services), 45-51.

Acquisitions Editors: Linda Anne Bump, PhD; Amy Pickering; **Developmental Editor:** Holly Gilly; **Assistant Editor:** Derek Campbell; **Copyeditor:** Kelly Winters; **Proofreader:** Pamela S. Johnson; **Indexer:** Marie Rizzo; **Permission Manager:** Dalene Reeder; **Graphic Designer:** Nancy Rasmus; **Graphic Artist:** Dawn Sills; **Cover Designer:** Nancy Rasmus; **Art Manager:** Craig Newsom; **Illustrator:** Dody Bullerman; **Printer:** Versa Press

Printed in the United States of America
10 9 8 7 6 5 4 3 2 1

Human Kinetics
Web site: www.humankinetics.com

United States: Human Kinetics
P.O. Box 5076
Champaign, IL 61825-5076
800-747-4457
e-mail: humank@hkusa.com

Canada: Human Kinetics
475 Devonshire Road Unit 100
Windsor, ON N8Y 2L5
800-465-7301 (in Canada only)
e-mail: orders@hkcanada.com

Europe: Human Kinetics
Units C2/C3 Wira Business Park
West Park Ring Road
Leeds LS16 6EB, United Kingdom
+44 (0) 113 278 1708
e-mail: hk@hkeurope.com

Australia: Human Kinetics
57A Price Avenue
Lower Mitcham, South Australia 5062
08 8277 1555
e-mail: liahka@senet.com.au

New Zealand: Human Kinetics
P.O. Box 105-231, Auckland Central
09-523-3462
e-mail: hkp@ihug.co.nz

CONTENTS

Appendix B   **Sample Performance Appraisal Forms and Checklists**   **141**

PREFACE

Sport organizations and their administrators have struggled in the past and will continue to grapple with performance appraisal. Even as athletic directors and other executive leaders in the sport delivery system stride confidently forward with more efficient, effective, and businesslike operations, an understanding of the dynamics of human resource management marks an area of deficiency. If sport organization administrators struggle with the demands of managing personnel in general, it is clear that the prospect of evaluating employee performance brings about a flurry of apprehension, discontent, and even fear. This is a major concern because the importance of effective performance appraisal is undisputed: the achievement of individual employees is directly linked to the organization's effectiveness or ability to achieve its goals; and along with being good for the organization, individual employees have a right to know how well they are doing at work in order to direct their activities toward career growth.

The dread with which managers and employees of sport organizations view performance appraisal must be reversed. This book provides the background, the procedures, and specific examples required for an understanding of performance appraisal and its use in sport organizations. It is the result of over a decade of personal interest and research in evaluating personnel in sport organizations, and years of practical application of performance appraisal concepts practiced in my role as a university athletic director.

The mind-set of the author bears further comment in order to establish context for this book. I believe in performance appraisal as a positive performance-management tool: an important contributor to success for both the organization *and* the employee. The true merit of an ongoing system of evaluation lies with its formative role: providing feedback that fosters motivation toward achievement. I see performance appraisal as a major change factor, a technique that contributes mightily to organizational culture regardless of the organization's size. I believe the development of job-specific evaluation criteria to be the single most important factor governing the entire performance appraisal system. After all, garbage in, garbage out!

This book is organized to provide a clear picture of the options available to enable managers to evaluate personnel, while advocating a specific method for establishing job-specific performance criteria and the use of a "management by objectives" goal-setting procedure. Chapter 1 provides an introduction to performance appraisal. The chapters that follow concentrate specifically on evaluating personnel in sport organizations. Chapter 2 focuses explicitly on evaluation criteria: why they are the cornerstone to effective evaluation; how to develop them for the specific job at hand; different types of criteria and advocacy for using a blending of them; the issues of measurability; and the criteria-training dyad. Chapter 3 details issues of appraisal procedure: how to build, implement, and optimize your system; who should perform the evaluation; when it should occur; and how to conduct an appraisal discussion. Chapter 4 presents the evaluation of different types of sport personnel (coaches, administrators, and so on) with a focus on the particular organizational setting (college or university, sport club, high school) in different countries. Chapter 5 covers other important performance appraisal issues such as achieving buy-in, unions, legal concerns, documentation, and advice on making the process work. Case studies are presented at the end of each chapter. The appendixes provide sample forms, checklists, and case study responses.

This book was written with two audiences in mind. First, managers in various types of sport organizations will be interested in the performance appraisal system championed here because it will provide them with a useful, step-by-step procedure for developing a new evaluation system or assessing one currently used in their organization. Second, professors and students in sport and recreation management will find this a useful reference text because it will ground them in performance appraisal research knowledge and provide them with development and installation tools for implementing a performance management system in the future. The book is intended to be practical, straightforward, and reader-friendly. Although the performance appraisal system advocated is grounded in the North American environment, it has wide-ranging applicability for evaluation development in sport organizations in other countries. Concrete examples of job descriptions, criteria development lists, checklists, and sample forms will also enable the reader to translate the book's content into actual use. Finally, this book is born out of a frustration that it does not already exist. The overwhelming uncertainty of sport managers looking for help developing appraisal criteria, and defining and implementing the overall evaluation system, is indicative of the absence of useful information. This book is an attempt to fill that void.

ACKNOWLEDGMENTS

My ability to complete a project of this magnitude was made possible with the help of many people. I am very fortunate to live and work in a tremendously supportive environment, in which my family, friends, and colleagues are a source of inspiration and unwavering support. Your interest, questions, and ideas had much to do with sustaining my motivation, and I thank you for this.

I am most grateful to Dr. P. Chelladurai and Dr. D. Zakrajsek from Ohio State University, who supported and nurtured my initial interest in this topic. I am thankful for the continuous support of Dr. John Corlett from the University of Windsor for his ideas and comments after reading the first draft of the manuscript. And I'm particularly indebted to Sheila Windle who provided both editorial and moral support for my writing by reviewing each draft of the manuscript, and who offered many good ideas regarding its content.

I also extend thanks to the staff of Human Kinetics who assisted with this project: Linda Bump, Amy Pickering, and especially Holly Gilly, who contributed many positive ideas to the completion of this project.

ONE

Evaluating Personnel in Sport Organizations: An Introduction

Carl grinds his teeth as he picks up the file on the corner of his desk. He's due in the small committee room in five minutes to conduct a performance appraisal interview with his ticket sales manager, Tom McLeod. Carl detests evaluation interviews. His palms begin to sweat as he recalls his last encounter—and the stuttering, wide-eyed, then tight-lipped employee who, as the 30-minute meeting progressed, displayed fear, disbelief, and then anger through watery eyes. It's great to convey positive feedback about work well done, but how in the world do you tell people that their work doesn't measure up? Carl leaves his office feeling that nothing good can possibly come from the meeting, which will undoubtedly be one-sided, tense, uncomfortable, and ineffective. He has a feeling that Tom McLeod is going to hate him by lunch time.

Down a floor, Tom is making his way to the stadium small committee room. His stomach is rumbling from the three cups of coffee he consumed this morning. As he walks, his temper flares with the inherent unfairness of it all. He thinks, *Carl won't know about the extra hours I've been putting in, nor will he comment on the effectiveness of my project work. In fact, Carl doesn't know anything about my work. I haven't even talked to Carl since my evaluation meeting a year ago. Carl has never come to discuss the implementation of my strategies; and he will have the nerve to comment on my effectiveness. I know what effectiveness means in the ivory tower—dollars raised by ticket sales. This is going to be brutal. I wonder if I should secretly tape record the interview.* Tom's hands are both cold and sweaty.

Such is the trepidation with which administrators and employees often view performance appraisal. But it need not be this way. This book focuses on ways to make performance appraisal more effective, comfortable, and communicative for both sport administrators and employees.

Worldwide, organized sport has become ingrained in many different cultures. Sport organizations of vastly different sizes and missions abound in countries around the globe, as illustrated by the number of nationalities pursuing Olympic gold medals and the growth of professionalism in various activities. Sport management as an area of study and professional delivery has kept pace by becoming increasingly sophisticated, in part by taking advantage of progress in the realm of business administration. Any organization, sport or otherwise, will exist and prosper only through the effective management of its resources.

The most important resources of any organization are its human resources. In a world fueled by technologies that contribute hugely to the efficiency of getting things done, the importance of the people who define and manage the material resources and technologies must not be underestimated. In a sport organization, the program managers, coaches, and other employees define the organization mission and play a critical role in the degree to which it is achieved. It stands to reason, then, that the development and performance of these employees, and the subsequent appraisal of their performance, are critically important for the organization's well-being.

Given such straightforward logic, why are the procedures commonly used for the evaluation of personnel in sport organizations in such disarray? Worse yet, why do many sport organizations not even bother to evaluate their personnel? And why is this scenario apparent in organizations all over the world, despite myriad and distinctive missions? Part of the reason is fear. Managers fear the reaction of the employee, while employees naturally fear the judgment of the manager. What if the appraisal does not take into account the employee's perception of true worth? Employees can feel vulnerable with their job security, promotions, salary increases, and other benefits hanging in the balance. Given that appraisal is emotionally charged to begin with, managers might naturally shy away from the conflict and the time involved. In addition, because of fear, people don't want to evaluate or be evaluated. Examples similar to the one in the following vignette ("Ineffective Performance Appraisal Communications") are common.

The managers in sport organizations are not alone in their trepidation regarding personnel evaluation. In organizations of various sizes and missions, performance appraisal is considered a difficult process, often poorly operationalized and poorly received. For decades, performance appraisal has been tolerated as a necessary evil at best. *Fortune* editor Walter Kiechel, as presented in Grote (1996), shares his ubiquitous opinion: "Let's be frank. Most managers hate conducting performance appraisals. If they think they can get away with it, they will skip such potential unpleasantness entirely. If compelled to go through the exercise, they tend to do so with

Ineffective Performance Appraisal Communications

Athletic director: "I'm not sure our newsletters are very effective." (He's thinking, *If you came to work at a decent time in the morning, you would meet your deadlines.*)

Sports information manager: "Well, they certainly cover all our sport areas." (He's thinking, *It's not my fault that none of the coaches give me decent story ideas.*)

Athletic director: "I liked what XYZ College produces." (He's thinking, *At least their people know how to string two coherent sentences together.*)

Sports information manager: "XYZ has fewer sports than us, and a great printing company to work with." (He's thinking, *Here we go—I'm overworked, underpaid, and the marketing manager can't cut a decent deal with a competent printing company. It's not my fault.*)

Athletic director: "What were our deadlines again for getting them in the mail?" (He's thinking, *I'll cut this guy some slack by just letting this go. He'll probably blow up and I'll end up having to get more involved.*)

Sports information manager: "August and January." (He's thinking, *Well that was a threat if I've ever heard one. This guy has had it in for me from day one. Why doesn't he like me?*)

Athletic director: "OK, that's about all I have for you." (He's thinking, *Thank heavens this is over.*)

bad grace, confusing the poor appraisee by mixing a kind of phony solicitousness with a candor that gives new meaning to the term 'brutal'" (p. ix).

As in many business organizations, the standards vary in the world of sport. But within many sport organizations the evaluation of personnel continues to range between not bothering to perform any specific evaluation to the zero-sum evaluation standards of winning versus losing. For example, coaches who produce winning teams are usually considered to be doing a good job; coaches whose teams lose are often not considered to be doing a good job. The world of sport, while having several zero-sum achievement factors such as win-loss outcomes, is not nearly this simplistic in reality, and such simplistic standards should not be used in evaluating achievement. Coaches who produce winning teams might actually do a poor job, and vice versa. Given all the trouble, potential pitfalls, and the resultant angst, why bother to conduct evaluations at all? Why is performance appraisal important to the sport organization?

Importance of Evaluating Staff

It is important to evaluate the staff of a sport organization for three basic reasons. First, the ultimate success of an organization is predicated on the quality and performance of its personnel. Although successful organizations are the product of many factors, it could be argued that the personnel defining, guiding, and implementing operations are the most important factors in the system. Second, it is impossible to manage an organization effectively without reliable information about people's work performance. Such information serves to maintain control of current operations and help guide future planning. Finally, sport organizations need performance appraisal because they are consumer-oriented organizations and because their consumers deserve quality.

However, that leads us to a more specific, and perhaps more compelling, reason to accurately and fairly evaluate personnel: because the employees deserve it. Performance appraisal is largely about communication, and employees deserve to know how well or how poorly they are doing in their jobs. They deserve regular and constructive feedback about how to succeed at work, improve their performance, and lead successful careers. For the employee, a lack of attention to performance problems can lead to dissatisfaction or apathy and eventually to job failure or withdrawal. I will go so far as to suggest that personnel deserve to be *coached*, and that employee success is a critical component feeding organizational success. This philosophy is congruent with the notion of *formative evaluation*, in which the specific purpose of the process is to provide constructive feedback, both positive and negative, to ensure employee success. It differs from *summative evaluation*, in which the bottom line of the evaluation is to address contract extension or remuneration issues. The importance of having a fair, well-defined, and easily operationalized performance appraisal system is discussed by Grote (1996): "Certainly judgments about how individuals are performing will be made whether or not there is a formal system. . . . But since many of these informal, spontaneous judgments will be erroneous, some formal procedure is needed to minimize the possibilities of bias and uninformed judgments" (pp. ix-x).

Performance Appraisal in the Context of Sport

It is critical that we understand the unique context of the sport setting and the impact it has for the management and evaluation of personnel. Unlike the company that builds "widgets" and has a work force devoted solely to either the production or sales of the "widget," sport organizations are often very diverse in the services or products they deliver, and therefore employ a rather diverse work force. A university athletic and recreation department will employ sport, fitness, and recreation personnel. The jobs of a coach, media manager, strength-training expert, dance instructor, and marketing manager are each unique positions that require specific job descriptions. The variety of jobs inherent to the mission of many sport organizations sets the appraisal of these personnel apart from the evaluation schemes employed within many other types of organizations. Under even closer scrutiny, it's apparent that many differences exist among the jobs performed within the sport organization. These variables, which tend to confound the situation, are some of the reasons that sport organizations have lagged behind in the development of effective employee performance appraisal. For example, should we evaluate the fitness instructor on how fit her class participants become; or how much they enjoy the class; or how many injuries are incurred from participation in the fitness class; or whether she can achieve a dedicated class following? This says nothing of her technical knowledge, administrative skill, or communication skills. Would we evaluate the athletic coach or the therapist on the same criteria? Would it be fair to suggest that the fitness instructor is ineffective at her job because some of the participants fail to reach certain fitness standards? What about the factors outside the control of the instructor, such as intensity of effort of the participant while exercising, or excessive fat intake through poor diet that leads to weight gain and hampers the participant's fitness progress? What effect do variables outside the control of the college athletic coach, such as an onslaught of midterm examinations just before playoff action, have on the success of the team? Would you evaluate an athletic therapist based on the successful rehabilitation rate of his patients if his only modalities of reconditioning are ice and ultrasound? The point is that employees of sport organizations often hold vastly different, and unique, positions.

Many unique variables might confound the context of the evaluation and make the appraisal of individuals within such positions a challenge. This fact is further exacerbated by the differences inherent to delivering sport for children versus elite sport versus the business of professional sport. A college sport therapist is different from a physiotherapist because of the nature of the usual injuries involved and because of the closed community of clientele that repeats itself. The profession of coaching is really vastly different from teaching although it certainly involves teaching; coaches spend a concentrated amount of time with their athletes imparting knowledge to enhance technical expertise and skill. However, they must also develop the team into a cohesive unit, and are held accountable to a much higher degree for the motivation and outcomes of the athletes and team. Many more examples of the unique state of the sport organization and the impact of such on the appraisal of personnel exist, and they will become apparent over the course of this book.

With due deference to the context in which sport organization employees perform their jobs, a system of performance appraisal must be defined and implemented. Over the past several decades, the world of business has steadily improved the evaluation process. It has evolved considerably from one-way communication between boss and subordinate to a more communicative and prescriptive process. During this same time, the performance appraisal process has become an established part of organizational life, definitely not some passing fad; and it is time for sport organizations to take advantage of the positive effects of performance appraisal. Let us take a closer look at both performance and appraisal.

What Is Performance?

Performance can be viewed as the activities or behaviors of workers completing tasks associated with a job. These behaviors, and the results or outcomes of such behaviors, are then assessed as to their appropriateness or desirability for the overall organization. For a college athletic team coach, behaviors associated with the job might include items such as game preparation, teaching techniques used at practice, or the motivation of athletes. It might also include the outcome of behaviors such as winning a certain number of games in a given season or attaining a specific overall team grade point average. The coach's level of achievement could be determined by comparing such criteria either to the behaviors of peer coaches or to a certain standard of performance. A community recreation director might perform such behaviors as planning, promoting, and delivering recreational programming. She or he might also be expected to achieve the outcomes of such behaviors as maintaining a break-even fiscal position or even making a profit. Criteria that evolve from actual behaviors attributed to a job include two categories:

1. Task-related criteria, which are directly related to the main task of the job (i.e., for the coach, items such as recruiting, planning, teaching, communicating, and making tactical decisions during competition; for the recreation director, features such as program design, market analysis, staff planning, scheduling, and budgeting).

2. Maintenance-related criteria, which are peripheral to the main task of the job (for either position, things such as being on time with paper work, establishing collegial working relationships with peers, and so on). Outcomes or results of behaviors are usually easily quantifiable items.

Chapter 2 will provide further detail on criteria types and information to help you develop job-specific criteria for evaluation.

Knowledge of what constitutes effective job performance is a critical building block in the establishment of solid performance appraisal systems. In other words, before an effective performance appraisal system can be developed and conducted, effective job performance must be clearly defined.

The Foundation of Performance Appraisal

Four critically important issues must be understood as the foundation of an evaluation system:

1. Performance appraisal is a process.
2. Organizational and contextual factors must be considered.
3. Jobs must be analyzed to determine criteria for evaluating performance.
4. An organization's mission guides the strategic activities of the organization.

Performance appraisal is not an isolated event that happens only at a specific time during the organizational cycle. Rather, it must be thought of as a process with several steps of events that occur in sequence. The process is one of communication and interchange, in which observed job behavior is discussed. The employee is motivated to achieve based on both informal and formal feedback. Most importantly, if the performance appraisal system is operationalized to occur only once a year, resulting in some paper work and a meeting, then the organization is losing a terrific opportunity to influence its own success, regardless of its mission. Well-managed organizations view performance appraisal as an ongoing process of communication in order to direct and motivate their employees. Feedback that's provided months after an incident has occurred may have little impact on the employee and represents a significant lost opportunity for corrective action.

As Murphy and Cleveland (1991) so accurately state, performance appraisal systems must be designed specifically for an organization because context is a very important factor. "Performance appraisal can not be adequately understood outside of its organizational context—the same appraisal system, the same criteria for evaluating ratings, the same rater-training programs, and so on are not the same if they exist in different contexts" (p. 25). The authors define contextual factors as a heterogeneous mix of factors that range from the social and legal system to the climate and culture within the organization. Such factors may occasionally impinge on the organization and the ability of individual employees to succeed at their jobs. Such factors need to be considered. Carroll and Schneier (1982) suggest that influences of the external environment might include the state of technological development, degree of competition, degree of unionization, economic conditions, or work force composition.

Influences internal to the organizational environment include organizational structure, a centralized or decentralized authority system, organizational size and policies, type of ownership, or work force values. Such contextual concerns need to be embraced by the performance appraisal system. The context of the sport environment that a coach works within is a good case in point. One would expect different performance rating criteria to be used in the evaluation of a professional coach versus collegiate coach versus minor league coach. Professional coaches might be held completely accountable for the team's performance, to the extent that winning and profit and fan numbers are prevalent in the coach's evaluation. The collegiate coach might work within an environment lacking a great facility, without scholarships to recruit top prospects, or sufficient full-time staff to help lead the program. The rating criteria within such a context might reasonably move from winning, profit, and fan support to graduation rates, student-athlete experience, and sound teaching practices. The minor league coach might be rated with a totally different set of criteria based on the standard that each child receives playing time and learns to enjoy both the game and rules of fair play.

When considering organizational contextual factors of the external and internal environment, one must also consider a further critical issue pertaining to the specificity of the performance appraisal. The single most important factor in constructing a fair and useful appraisal system is the development of job-specific performance criteria that constitute the critical mass of what is evaluated. Although it is important to articulate the purpose, timing, method, and standards of the evaluation process, it is crucial to first define *performance.* There is little utility in accurately measuring someone's job performance if the criteria measured are unrelated or inconsequential to the job. Job-specific performance criteria emanate from a process of job analysis that helps to define job descriptions. Criteria appropriate for the evaluation of an employee must be derived directly from the employee's job description. This process is discussed in detail in chapter 2.

Finally, the need for a performance appraisal *system* and the importance of organizational *context* and the development of *job-specific performance criteria* must be in congruence with the mission of the organization. That is, the organization must have a clearly defined mission, and this mission statement must guide the strategic activities of the organization and its employees. If the organization can't chart its future direction by defining its mission, then even the best efforts of its employees will not ensure success.

Approaches to Performance Appraisal

Having discussed some of the broad issues that affect the development and implementation of a performance appraisal system, we will briefly define several approaches commonly used for appraising performance. Before we begin, however, it is important to note that rarely is any one of these approaches used in isolation. Rather, most organizations incorporate components of any number of different approaches in the development of their own specific procedures. Although several unique approaches will be reviewed, the rest of this book will articulate and advocate one procedure that I recommend, based on research and personal experience, as the most appropriate for the assessment of personnel in sport organizations. This procedure is commonly known as management by objectives (MBO). It involves a procedure of goal setting with individual employees and then rating performance against previously set and agreed-on criteria along with the achievement of employee goals. It is a system that encourages open, two-way communication between manager and subordinate. MBO is particularly well suited for use within sport organizations because they usually involve the assessment of limited numbers of personnel, and because the sporting context is unusually attuned to setting goals.

Dick Grote, in *The Complete Guide to Performance Appraisal* (1996), suggested that there are four components that make up job performance: the performer, the situation, resultant behaviors, and the results of such behaviors. Grote further suggests that the approaches used over the years to assess performance have focused on these four components.

Focus on the Performer

Older approaches to performance appraisal that focused on the performer were called *trait-based systems.* These largely archaic systems focused on the development of a listing of traits or personal attributes that were assumed to result in good job performance. These types of systems stressed not what the employee did or produced, but what kind of person the employee was. Such systems may still exist in some organizations, but a focus on what an employee *is* as opposed to what he or she *does* is largely outdated and does not predict successful performance. Given that trait-based data provide little ammunition for change and little reflection on actual job achievement (in addition to the fact that they are unlikely to survive legal scrutiny) this system is not recommended for use.

Focus on the Situation

Although situational analysis may be important in assessing overall job performance, an appraisal that only defines the situation under which the employee operates is obviously ludicrous. Open-ended essay-type evaluations sometimes erroneously focus heavily on the situation at hand. For example, the facilities available to a recreation director could easily unduly influence the director's evaluation. However, whether a recreation director must work with inadequate facilities or with excellent facilities should not override the importance of evaluating how well the recreation director performs with the facilities that do exist. Is this person being fairly assessed for achievement notwithstanding the facilities available for programming? A focus on the situation should only provide complementary and secondary information to the behaviors or results of behaviors assessed.

Focus on Behaviors

Behavior-based appraisals focus on what the person does, or the actions and abilities displayed while the person completes the tasks of the job. Such a focus aligns with previous sections of this chapter that detail the importance of defining job-specific performance criteria. Many of these criteria must be behavior-based, detailing optimal modes of performance to ensure success on the job. Assessment forms that use rating scales or checklist methods are commonly used to assess an individual's success at achieving specific performance criteria against norms or descriptions of successful performance.

Rating scales might use a continuum of assessment judgment (excellent to unacceptable; always to never) or discrete categories (superior, good, satisfactory, unsatisfactory). The most commonly used rating scales ("Examples of Rating Scales," pages 12-13), briefly described, include the following:

- **Numerically anchored or summated rating scale** (example *a*): A questionnaire with a rating scale for which raters are asked to mark the point or number on the scale that marks their evaluation of the degree of performance on a specific criterion. Usually a set of several such scales are used with different dimensions or topics of criteria listed. Such groupings of criteria may be ranked in order of importance, and it is customary to average the ratings within each scale (see Landy & Farr, 1980, 1982 for further detail).

- **Adjective-anchored or graphic rating scale** (example *b*): Similar to the numerical rating scale, except that adjectives, not numbers, are used to anchor the points on the scale.

- **Behaviorally anchored rating scale** (BARS; example *c*): Another appraisal technique incorporating several performance dimensions or scales, a BARS evaluation form is usually arranged vertically on a page, with a different page for each criterion under evaluation. Usually one or more statements appear beside each of the scale points, which are brief descriptions of actual worker behavior that illustrate job performance at each level on the scale. These behavioral statements anchor the scale at each point, thus the name *behaviorally anchored rating scale*. If a job assessment produced eight dimensions under assessment, then eight separate BARS scales would comprise the appraisal form, each broken into several (usually five to nine) behavioral statements. Raters would mark the appropriate scale value opposite the anchor that best describes the ratee's performance. BARS involves a higher level of sophistication and specificity than numerical or graphic rating scales (see Smith & Kendall, 1963, who developed BARS; see also Carroll & Schneier, 1982; Grote, 1996).

- **Behavioral observation scale** (BOS; example *d*): Sometimes referred to as behavioral frequency scale, this system is similar to BARS, but the questionnaire is designed to collect the frequency with which job incumbents engage in behaviors using a Likert-type scale (e.g., very frequently to never; almost always to almost never). Numerical values are given to the frequency descriptors and often averaged to provide an overall rating value (see Latham & Wexley, 1981).

Examples of Rating Scales

a Numerically Anchored (Summated) Rating Scale

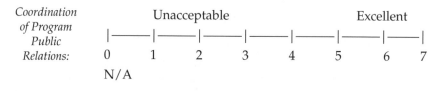

Coordination
of Program
Public
Relations:

Unacceptable   Excellent

|—|—|—|—|—|—|—|
0   1   2   3   4   5   6   7

N/A

b Adjective-Anchored (Graphic) Rating Scale

Being on
Time With
Paper Work

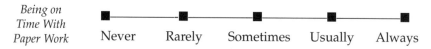

Never   Rarely   Sometimes   Usually   Always

c Behaviorally Anchored Rating Scale

Game Day Coaching Effectiveness:

*Extremely
Good
Performance*

7   Has game plan prepared and effectively communicated to athletes; projects calm and confidence; demonstrates effective tactical maneuvering; communicates directly to athletes often during competition; total team effort results in a competitive result.

6   Substitutes effectively as a result of competitive factors; successfully adapts to opposing coaches' tactics and strategies; has a better team by the end of the competition; athletes show positive response to coach; coach positively reinforces all forms of effort, whether resulting in good or bad result.

5   Athletes are sometimes responsive to the coach's interventions; the coach shows frustration infrequently; every attempt is made to adapt game plans when not working.

4   The coach makes an effort to cheer on all athletes; often tactical decision-making and interventions are unsuccessful; the coach may display negative body language and rarely communicates with players leaving the game.

3   The coach sometimes loses composure; has a tendency to overcoach with bombardment of tactical details during the game and in time-outs; athletes

often react with little excitement and are sometimes completely unresponsive; the coach often appears tired and disillusioned about the prospects for the season.

2   The coach takes regular technical or unsportsmanlike penalties, and has a propensity to yell at officials; athletes' conduct becomes increasingly argumentative and aggressive toward coaches and officials; the coach loses composure often and positive interaction with athletes becomes rare.

1   The coach is unprepared, uninvolved, and appears disinterested; often shows up late; is uncommunicative and unhelpful in all aspects of the job.

Extremely Poor
Performance

d   Behavioral Observation Scale

The Sports Information Officer ...

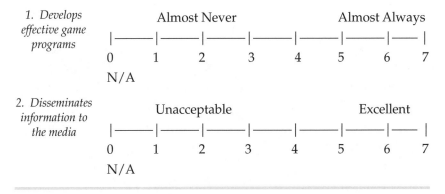

Checklists ("Examples of Checklists," pages 14-15) are another method sometimes used in evaluation. They are similar to rating scales. Checklists contain several items describing desirable behavior on the job. Raters are asked to check those that apply to the incumbent. Several items can be checked from one list that is developed to represent the possible behaviors of an employee.

The most commonly used checklists include the following:

- **Adjective checklists** (example *a*): Such checklists might contain a set of adjectives that describe a worker's behavior; each adjective checked gives one point. Checklists might also contain statements of worker behavior. An average value of all items checked provides the overall score.

- **Critical incidents checklists** (example *b*): Similar to the procedure listed for adjective checklists; incidents are developed that discriminate between successful and unsuccessful performance, and raters indicate which incidents are observed for each ratee.

- **Forced choice checklists** (example *c*): For these checklists, raters are forced to choose between the available alternatives to describe the behavior of an employee, whether favorable or not. The rater is allowed to choose one response, and several scales are usually presented to the evaluator. This method was developed to correct for rater errors such as central tendency and leniency (for more information check Blum & Naylor, 1968).

Examples of Checklists

a Adjective Checklist

Position: _____

Articulate	_____	Respected	_____
Knowledgeable	_____	Task-oriented	_____
Decisive	_____	Organized	_____
Good leader	_____	Takes initiative	_____
Strong motivator	_____	Good communicator	_____
Punctual	_____	Reasonable	_____
Gets results	_____	Good planner	_____
Good budgeter	_____	Evaluates effectively	_____
Cooperative	_____	Well known	_____
Professional	_____	Total:	_____

b Critical Incidents Checklist

Position: _____

_____ Unable to define or communicate the team mission for game or season.

_____ Often appears late, disorganized, and disinterested.

_____ Omits important information when teaching or communicating strategy.

_____ Is a cheerleader more often than a strategist.

_____ Substitutes effectively to change the course of the game.

_____ Effectively communicates feedback to athletes that produces results.

_____ Controls the game through tactical maneuvering.

_____ Expertly devises and communicates a superior game plan that frequently produces goal acquisition.

c Forced Choice Checklist

Position: _____

_____ 1. Has excellent knowledge of sport marketing and can effectively communicate such knowledge to the students in our employ.

_____ 2. Endeavors to remain current and develop strategy specific to the situation.

_____ 3. Is always prepared and on time for meetings.

_____ 4. Seeks the advice and feedback of sponsors regularly.

Focus on Results of Behaviors

Results-based appraisals focus on the outcomes of what the person does or the achievements displayed once the tasks of the job are completed. Two main approaches to evaluation exist that focus heavily on outcomes or results of behaviors: the accountabilities and measures approach (Grote, 1996), and the management by objectives approach (Drucker, 1954). They are described briefly in the following paragraphs.

- **Accountabilities and measures approach:** This method of appraisal is a results-based approach in which objectives mandated for employee achievement are defined by the organization's central management, along with the measures or performance standards for each objective. This controlling and objective measurement style is used to ensure that goals and standards of achievement are well-communicated. This system is likely to set performance criteria that mirror the job description. It differs from other results-oriented evaluation systems in its top-down implementation approach, which precludes employee input to its development.

- **Management by objectives (MBO):** MBO is a performance appraisal system and a complete philosophy of management that involves a system of results-oriented goal setting. The important distinction between MBO and the accountabilities approach mentioned previously is the complete involvement of the employee in determining the goals to be achieved, and the ongoing demands for communication between manager and employee. The system is job-specific; relies on open communication and the coaching skills of the manager; focuses on future results and how to achieve them; and attempts to provide a proactive, challenging, yet positive work environme nt. MBO will be discussed in much greater detail in chapter 3.

In summary, the preceding sections briefly identified approaches to performance appraisal that focused on one of the four elements of the person in the job. Two important points should be remembered: First, most performance appraisal systems developed by organizations are hybrids that use several of the approaches defined previously in the development of a system specific to their needs. Second, some organizations evaluate using a more global or overall achievement approach.

Focus on Overall Achievement

One open-ended example of the overall achievement method involves the narrative essay. This approach to performance appraisal involves the rater describing both the strengths and weaknesses of the employee, achievements within the performance period, and a prescription for future success. Tremendous latitude is given the rater with respect to what is appraised and discussed within the evaluation. The method can provide deep and insightful assessments of performance if the rater is knowledgeable about appraisal and a skilled writer. At the same time, rater bias and reliability are major concerns. The evaluation may also suffer if the rater is not a good writer. Another example of an overall achievement method is the ranking of employees. Ranking compares the job incumbent's performance to others in similar positions, as opposed to comparisons to standards of performance. This technique ensures that job incumbents will be globally compared and that differentiation among employees will result.

The most commonly used ranking techniques ("Examples of Ranking Methods," pages 18-19) include the following:

- **Simple ranking** (example *a*): With consideration for overall performance in mind, raters simply rank order all employees. Sometimes more than one person performs the ranking and average scores are used. The simplicity of the method, although considered a strength by some, is of concern given the lack of actual criteria and the difficulties that can arise when raters feel no difference exists between employees.

- **Paired comparisons** (example *b*): All job incumbents are paired and compared. A point is given for each comparison won on the basis of overall performance.

- **Forced distribution ranking** (example *c*): A number of categories of performance are defined, for example Excellent, Good, Fair, and Unacceptable. The rater may then be expected to force 20 percent of employees into each of the highest and lowest categories, and divide the remainder within the two middle categories. This assumes that the performance of the group corresponds to a normal distribution curve—an assumption that may not be accurate. The strength of forced distribution ranking is that it can help to alleviate errors of central tendency and leniency (described in chapter 5).

I do not recommend ranking as a performance appraisal tool for sport organizations. I've found the jobs of sport personnel to be too distinctive to enable fair comparisons among people within different positions. This seems to be the case even when comparing coaches of different teams. So many contextual factors exist that fair comparisons are almost impossible.

Some Final Thoughts on the Overall Objective

Regardless of the type of evaluation system developed, or the complexity or size of the organization involved, several factors may have positive effects on the performance appraisal system and can help make it a successful and important performance management tool for the organization. Left unmanaged, the same factors may reduce the entire process to a colossal waste of time. Keep the following points in mind.

The performance appraisal system must

- be job-specific at every level of assessment for every employee assessed,
- be operationalized by those with sufficient and appropriate training to ensure that the system works effectively,
- be accepted and committed to by both raters and ratees,
- have buy-in from top-level executives in the organization,
- allow for an appeal process,
- endeavor to ensure accuracy and negate bias,
- be legally defensible and comply with organizational policy, and
- integrate with other human resource management systems used by the organization.

Examples of Ranking Methods

a Simple Ranking

Position: _____   Date: _____

Prepared by:_____

_____ M. Morrison   _____ J.P. Turner

_____ T. Walker   _____ J.R. Turner

_____ S. Laframboise   _____ B. Roots

_____ T. McKay   _____ A. Bernard

b Paired Comparison Ranking

Position:_____   Date: _____

Prepared by:_____

Ranking #1

_____ M. Morrison

_____ J.P. Turner

_____ M. Morrison

_____ T. Walker

_____ M. Morrison

_____ J.R. Turner

_____ M. Morrison

_____ S. Laframboise

_____ M. Morrison

_____ B. Roots

_____ M. Morrison

_____ T. McKay

_____ M. Morrison

_____ A. Bernard

Ranking #2

_____ J.P. Turner

_____ T. Walker

_____ J.P. Turner

_____ J.R. Turner

_____ J.P. Turner

_____ S. Laframboise

_____ J.P. Turner

_____ B. Roots

_____ J.P. Turner

_____ T. McKay

_____ J.P. Turner

_____ A. Bernard

Ranking #3

_____ T. Walker

_____ J.R. Turner

_____ T. Walker

_____ S. Laframboise

_____ T. Walker

Ranking #4

_____ J.R. Turner

_____ S. Laframboise

_____ J.R. Turner

_____ B. Roots

_____ J.R. Turner

_____	B. Roots	_____	T. McKay
_____	T. Walker	_____	J.R. Turner
_____	T. McKay	_____	A. Bernard
_____	T. Walker		
_____	A. Bernard		

Ranking #5		**Ranking #6**	
_____	S. Laframboise	_____	B. Roots
_____	B. Roots	_____	T. McKay
_____	S. Laframboise	_____	B. Roots
_____	T. Mckay	_____	A. Bernard
_____	S. Laframboise		
_____	A. Bernard		

Ranking #7

_____	T. McKay	_____	A. Bernard

Ranking Totals (must equal 28):

_____	M. Morrison	_____	J.P. Turner
_____	T. Walker	_____	J.R. Turner
_____	S. Laframboise	_____	B. Roots
_____	T. McKay	_____	A. Bernard

c Forced Distribution Ranking

Department Employee List:

M. Morrison	J.R. Turner	T. McKay
J.P. Turner	S. Laframboise	A. Bernard
T. Walker	B. Roots	

Unacceptable 20% (1-2)	Fair	Good	Excellent 20% (1-2)
J.P. Turner	S. Laframboise	T. Walker	B. Roots
		T. McKay	A. Bernard
		M. Morrison	
		J.R. Turner	

Summary

This chapter provided a brief introduction to performance appraisal. The importance of evaluating personnel and defining the notion of performance are emphasized. We've also discussed the foundation that successful procedures for evaluating employee performance are based on and outlined several approaches commonly used for appraising performance. In addition, we've considered actual techniques used for employee performance appraisal, as well as several important factors that may help guide the process. These topics provide the basic knowledge necessary for a discussion of performance appraisal criteria, the topic of chapter 2.

IN THE MANAGER'S SHOES

How in the World Do I Get Started?

David Carrington landed his dream job as athletic director as St. Jessop's College six months ago. As expected, David's first months on the job were action-packed. He was busy meeting people, learning about programs, and getting to know the intricacies of the job. During a lull in the action between school semesters, David has time to focus on the evaluation function of managing his employees. However, he is unclear about the procedures in place for evaluating his staff, and so he visits his superior to ask specifically about the performance appraisal system used at St. Jessop's. His superior, the dean of students, can only point to an evaluation form used to assess classroom teaching. With support for David's interest in effectively evaluating staff, she sends him to the human resources department, where David is amazed to learn that no such system exists for the athletic department. Worse yet, upon further investigation, David finds that the human resources department at the college consists of three individuals, two of whom can offer no advice, while the other member is off sick on long-term disability. Realizing that no help is forthcoming from the college administration, David returns to his office to consider his options.

With pen and paper in front of him, David begins to define his options, an exercise he completes regularly when confronted with a difficult problem. He considers his human resource responsibilities as athletic director. The athletic department has 11 employees: an athletic program manager, five sport team head coaches, an athletic therapist, a sport information manager, a ticket manager, a travel manager, and a secretary. The options are clearly to perpetuate the status quo by doing nothing, or to try to develop an evaluation protocol that will aid in David's management of the department. David quickly decides that he must develop a method of performance appraisal for his department. It is an easy choice given the obvious benefits for staff development and performance management. What steps should David follow to get started?

Creating an Acceptance of Change

The Silverwood Sport and Recreation Center (SSRC) is a multi-sport facility located within the heart of the city. The facility is 27 years old and has 94 full-time employees who manage the complex and deliver programs within the ice rink, stadium, gymnasiums, and pool. Employees are divided into eight departments, each of which is led by a managing director. Amazingly, half of the organization's employees have worked at SSRC for their entire career, between 16 and 27 years. Each department employs between 7 and 11 persons, and 59 percent of the employees are male.

Christine Stapleton is the chief executive officer of the facility. Upon finishing her third year with the organization, Christine becomes concerned that the personnel management system is out of date and that the employees of SSRC are "in a rut," so to speak. She perceives a growing resistance among the front-line employees to just about any form of change associated with management systems in both the facility and program delivery areas. Christine worries that the organization is missing an important opportunity to motivate and energize staff through employee goal setting. Although she is convinced that a new performance management system must be developed, Christine is worried about the lack of initiative among the employees at almost every level. She knows that the answer to the question "Should we create a new performance management system?" is an emphatic "yes." She worries that selling the concept to members of her organization will be more difficult, especially given the current laid-back internal climate and the length of time many of SSRC's employees have been on the job.

Christine must define her change strategy. She realizes that her first task is to convince the department heads of the need for change. She decides that part of creating an acceptance of change in performance management can be achieved through weekly management meetings in group and individual settings. Christine also concludes that the ammunition for creating the change will come from a comprehensive paperwork audit to solicit ideas from her current managers about using the evaluation system as is.

Her task, then, is twofold: Christine must

1. define the questions of a paperwork audit to collect information from her managers about using the current performance appraisal system; and

2. develop a rating scale survey to gain an accurate picture of the views of a stratified sample of employees across the organization.

What questions might be posed in each of these data collection phases? See appendix C for reflections on the cases.

Performance Appraisal Criteria: What Should Be Evaluated?

TWO

Clearly, the most important components in the design of a performance appraisal system are the criteria on which the evaluation will be made. Assessing how well an individual is doing a job requires that the job and expectations be clearly defined. In any assessment of performance, criteria specific to the desired outcome must be the basis of the investigation. Otherwise, decisions are made arbitrarily, a method of objectively documenting events is not established, and bias or unrelated factors drive the assessment. The identification of appropriate criteria for evaluation sets the stage for the evaluation by serving as an operational definition of successful performance (Ilgen & Barnes-Farrell, 1984; Levy, 1989).

Criteria are performance expectations, usually grouped into evaluative dimensions, that define standards against which job factors will be measured. Early on in the development of such performance appraisal systems it was suggested that such criteria might include items reflective of the ratee's skills, abilities, knowledge, behaviors, motives, or attributes (Smith, 1976). More recently, Campbell's theory of performance, as presented in Chelladurai (1999), defined several domains important for evaluation. The main categories

23

included Job-Specific Task Performance, including written and oral communication, supervision and leadership, and management and administration; Non-Job-Specific Task Performance, involving effort, personal discipline, and facilitation of peer and team performance; and Citizenship Behaviors, such as conscientiousness, courtesy, and altruism. Research conducted in conjunction with two of my colleagues (MacLean & Zakrajsek, 1994, 1996; and MacLean & Chelladurai, 1995) defined performance in terms of behaviors and designated categories relative to assessment. *Behavioral process factors* were defined as those behaviors actually performed on the job. *Behavioral product factors* were defined as the result produced by the process factors. More specific information regarding individual types of evaluation criteria will follow in the next section.

Before we delve deeper into the detail of evaluation criteria and their development, several critical points warrant further and immediate comment (Ilgen & Barnes-Farrell, 1984). First, the criteria for performance appraisal must be relevant to the job and represent aspects of performance that actually differentiate between effective and ineffective work. Next, these criteria should be free from deficiency, representing all relevant aspects of work performance. In addition, good criteria are reliable, representing performance dimensions that consistently differentiate between good and bad performance. Also, criteria should be free from contamination, meaning that the criteria chosen must be taken in the context of the environment of the position being evaluated. Finally, performance appraisal criteria are specific to the job under scrutiny; so specific in fact that the criteria must be representative of the actual job description for the position under evaluation (Deets & Tyler, 1986; Ilgen & Barnes-Farrell, 1984; Murphy & Cleveland, 1991; Sashkin, 1981). With this information in mind, let us investigate the possible types of criteria that might be used to evaluate the employees of a sport organization.

Categories of Performance Appraisal Criteria

As stated in chapter 1, performance appraisal systems developed over the years have focused almost exclusively on one of the following: the performer, the situation, the employee's behaviors, or the results of employee behaviors. The general typologies of criteria used within such evaluation schemes have naturally followed suit. Each of these one-dimensional approaches has its associated pitfalls. Specifically, the sole use of criteria that focus on the performer, usually termed trait criteria, is not recommended because in most cases the intent of the evaluation is to assess what the person does in the job, not what kind of person he or she may be. Assessing the fitness instructor on how he looks as opposed to what he teaches would obviously lead to spurious outcomes. The same can be said for using criteria that focus mainly on the situation, as the situation may or may not be relevant to the performance of the individual. A fitness instructor should not be rated solely on the facilities in which she works. Such a focus on the instructor's surroundings is misleading because it likely falls outside the control of the instructor and has little impact on how well the individual teaches the fitness class. Rather than focusing on the traits of the individual under evaluation, or the situation the person is working within, performance appraisal criteria should emanate from the behavior of the employee under evaluation. This line of reasoning has resulted in the generation of the final two categories of focus. These categories include an emphasis on assessing performer behaviors related to the job, and on assessing the results of those behaviors, as originally defined in the work of James (1973) and Smith (1976), respectively. This focus on behaviors continues to be advocated and will provide the solution to defining criteria appropriate for job-specific performance appraisal.

Behavioral Process Factors

Behavioral process factors are the actual behaviors performed by the employee while on the job. For an athletic coach, behavioral process factors would include criteria that focus on the actual process of coaching, as opposed to the outcomes or results of coaching, the situations, or the personality traits of the coach. Criteria for this situation might include items like the coach's ability to communicate effectively with athletes, evidence of strong planning, the use of effective teaching methodology, and level of understanding of appropriate age-group skills, instead of the ultimate win-loss criterion. In another example, a recreation director might be expected to perform the following job-related behaviors that are process factors: scheduling and facility management; record keeping and inventory database; program evaluation; and training and supervision of instructors. Both examples serve to illustrate that behavioral process factors are the actual behaviors completed while executing tasks of the job in question. Under further scrutiny it is apparent that process factors easily subdivide into two separate types, defined as *task-related* and *maintenance-related* (MacLean, 1992).

Task-related behavioral process factors include criteria reflecting actual job behaviors that are directly associated with the main task of the job. For the coach, this would include criteria items that are most specific to actual coaching, such as practice management or quality of interaction with athletes. For the position of recreation director, task-related behavioral process factors would involve job-specific criteria such as program development and scheduling. Both of these sets of criteria are in contrast to *maintenance-related* behavioral process factors, which include items peripheral to the main task of the job, but nonetheless important precursors to success, such as working relationships with coworkers, interaction with the public or media, and timeliness with paper work. Both the coach and recreation director should be assessed on items peripheral to the main tasks of their jobs, such as those listed previously, because from a global perspective, they are important elements of the working environment of the organization.

In summary, this section describes two main types of evaluation criteria important for use in a performance appraisal system, which reflect actual behaviors necessary to complete the main *task* of a job, and actual behaviors required to *maintain* the work environment. It is crucial that both of these criteria types be reflected within the arsenal of criteria used to assess an individual's job performance, no matter what job is under scrutiny. In addition to task- and maintenance-related behavioral process factors, a third type of criterion is used in performance appraisal. It involves *behavioral product factors*, the outcomes of those criteria listed previously.

Behavioral Product Factors

Behavioral product factors include criteria that are outcomes or results of behaviors performed on the job. These can be negative or positive indicators that are usually quantifiable. For the athletic coach, behavioral product factors would include items such as win-loss record, the number of "blue-chip" athletes recruited in a given season, or performance improvements of athletes from season to season. For the recreation director, product factors might include assessing the job incumbent on participant numbers in specific program categories over a period of time, or the individual's record for developing new programs. Behavioral product factors are the natural end result precipitated by the performance of the job incumbent while performing the main tasks of the job.

Although it is often easy to focus on criteria such as product factors because they are so easily quantifiable, caution is recommended whenever too much emphasis is placed on one type of criteria. Table 2.1 provides a summary of performance appraisal criteria categories for the examples of athletic coach and recreation director.

Which Category of Criteria Should Be Used?

No single category of criteria is considered adequate to evaluate employees. Rather, it is recommended that a variety of task-related

Table 2.1   Example Performance Appraisal Criteria By Categories

	Coach	Recreation Director
Behavioral product factors	Win-loss record Number of blue-chip athletes recruited Athlete performance improvement from season to season Coach's invited public appearances Making the playoffs	Number of participants in programs Participant satisfaction average scores Record of new program development Yearly profit margin Balanced male/female programming
Behavioral process factors—task-related	Ability to communicate with athletes Utilizing effective game tactics & strategies Scouting opponents Recruiting quality athletes Effective teaching methods	Effective programming to meet participant interest Strong planning Meaningful training of volunteers Adequate supervision of weight room area Effective program evaluation
Behavioral process factors—maintenance-related	Complying with organization's philosophy Working effectively with staff members Involvement with professional association Adhering to budget Monitoring athlete eligibility	Purchasing equipment Attending conferences and appropriate workshops Adhering to budget Involvement with professional association Coordination of publicity and effective public relations

process factors, maintenance-related process factors, and product factors make up the criteria used to evaluate an employee. Furthermore, the criteria developed must be specific to the position under assessment. I make this recommendation, along with a host of other researchers, because an appraisal system that is based solely on one type of criteria is both deficient and extremely short-sighted (Brief, 1998; Buford, Burkhalter, & Jacobs, 1988; Carroll & Schneier, 1982; Landy & Farr, 1983; Murphy & Cleveland, 1991; Saal & Knight, 1995; Schuler & Jackson, 1996).

The use of task-related process factors makes easy conceptual sense because such items most closely reflect what the job incumbent actually does. The use of results of behaviors is also easily understood because a natural relationship exists between an employee getting results and the organization meeting its goals. Murphy and Cleveland (1991), however, wisely advise that too much emphasis on results makes it difficult to determine what is being evaluated—the person or the situation in which he or she works: "Results-oriented criteria can lead supervisors and subordinates to ignore a wide range of behaviors (e.g., maintaining good interpersonal relations) that are critical to the survival and effectiveness of the organization but are not uniquely tied to any given product or result" (p. 92). Landy and Farr (1983) suggest that appraisals that rely solely on outcome measures result in a dysfunctional work environment because maximizing outcomes becomes the only organizational goal. This leads to a "cutthroat" atmosphere at work. As discussed by MacLean and Chelladurai (1995) in their article "Dimensions of Coaching Performance," this particular concern is exacerbated in the case of coaching evaluation because coaches are engaged in zero-sum games. That is, every game has to produce a winner and a loser no matter how close the contest may be. Thus, an extremely well-coached and thus excellent performance may enter the appraisal system as a negative when only results-based criteria are used.

Maintenance-related process factors fill the gap mentioned previously by rewarding behaviors that help sustain positive, team-oriented working conditions. Consider the strength and conditioning coach of an Olympic swimming team. It is counterproductive to evaluate this coach solely on the outcomes of training measured by strength gain because in doing so the importance of drug- and injury-free, sport-specific strength training may be missed. So might the importance of teaching the athlete proper technique to enable training without supervision, effective communication with the coaching staff, favorable interaction and integration of programming with the other sport science professionals consulting the team to prevent overtraining, and other factors. Each of these issues is critical to the successful performance of the strength coach and must be included in the criteria that measure ultimate job performance.

Having emphasized the importance of using a variety of different types of evaluation criteria, we will move forward to discuss a procedure for defining job-specific performance appraisal criteria.

The Development of Job-Specific Performance Appraisal Criteria

Building on the assertion that three main categories of appraisal criteria exist and that a mixture of each of the three should be used within the performance appraisal system, figure 2.1 presents a comprehensive model for the development of job-specific performance appraisal criteria. The model, one that I first introduced to sport management in 1993 (MacLean, 1993), is a literature-based theoretical model developed to respond to the question, "What criteria should be used for the appraisal of an individual in a specific job?" The stepwise procedure involves (a) job assessment, which leads to (b) the creation of the job description, which contributes to (c) the definition of the domain of performance. The domain of performance comprises behavioral product and process factors, as described previously. Also considered in the development of the individual criteria are the influences of both the external and internal organizational environment.

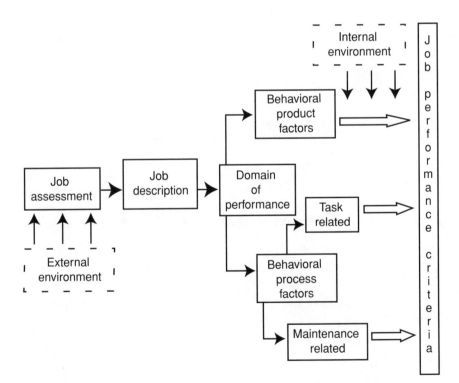

Figure 2.1   Comprehensive model for the development of job-specific performance appraisal criteria.

Step 1: Complete a Job Assessment

Ivancevich and Glueck (1989) define job assessment as a process used to outline the specific tasks, behaviors, and responsibilities needed to perform a job successfully. The purpose is to identify acceptable levels of performance for a job; this is achieved through repeated observation and study (Byars & Rue, 1979). The result is a list of tasks that make up the job and help to determine the duties, skills, responsibilities, working conditions, and, where appropriate, personal characteristics applicable to successful performance. Once completed, the job assessment will provide specific job-related information that must be articulated within the job description. For example, for the position of university athletic coach, a job assessment will help delineate the tasks and behaviors performed by individual coaches that are valued by an organization and its employees. The list of tasks can be generated by comparison to similar jobs, by interviewing job incumbents, by observation, or by asking the job incumbent to keep a log of activities. An example of a job analysis performed for a university women's basketball coach begins at the bottom of the page. Another example, this time illustrating job analysis for a high school athletic director, begins on page 32. Along with performance indicators that reflect the organization's desired outcomes as illustrated for the coach and athletic director in the examples provided, the job assessment acts as a precursor to the development of the written job description.

Job Analysis

Position: *Head Women's Basketball Coach*   Department: *Athletics*

Reports to: *Director of Athletics*

Responsible for: Leadership, vision, and overall development of all aspects of the women's basketball program

Specifics of this position include:

Coaching in practice sessions	Coaching in games or competitions
1. Knowledge of sport	9. Developing effective game plans
2. Teaching	10. Professional conduct
3. Practice planning	11. Employing useful tactics
4. Motivating	12. Making decisions
5. Management of discipline	13. Coach demeanor

6. Knowledge and application of training principles

7. Effective communication

8. Skill and movement analysis

14. Appearance and team conduct

15. Use of all personnel

Administrative tasks	Philosophy
16. Competitive scheduling	24. Compliance with institution's philosophy
17. Purchase and care of equipment	25. Adhering to rules and regulations
18. Planning and organizing	26. Concern for athlete as person and student
19. National/league meeting attendance	27. Support for total athletic program
20. Athlete eligibility	28. Consistent, fair athlete treatment
21. Maintaining statistics	29. Safety of participants
22. Adhering to budget	30. Demonstration of sportsmanship
23. Productive management of time	

Public relations	Recruiting
31. Media liaison	36. Developing the recruiting plan
32. Public speaking	37. Home and campus visits
33. Liaison with high school coaches	38. Scouting and identification
34. Summer camps	39. Formation of recruitment network
35. Offering clinics	40. Closing the deal

Personal performance characteristics

41. Working relationships with peers

42. Professional conduct

(continued)

(continued)

43. Punctuality
44. Complete, accurate, and on-time paper work
45. Appropriate dress for practices and games
46. Commitment

Job Analysis

Position: *High School Athletic Director*   Department: *Physical Education*

Reports to: *School Principal*

Responsible for: Leadership and organization of all aspects of the school sports program

Specifics of this position include:

Organization	Planning
1. Knowledge of sport	9. Game schedules
2. Making travel arrangements	10. Practice schedules
3. Training student workers	11. Budget projections
4. Scheduling student workers	12. Hosting of events
5. League management	13. Use of personnel
6. Purchase of equipment	14. Staffing
7. Inventory and storage of equipment	15. Developing rules policy
8. Home event management	

Evaluation	Leadership
16. Training of personnel	22. Philosophical orientation
17. Appraisal of personnel	23. Equity for girls and boys programs
18. Supervision of personnel	24. Overall policy development
19. Assessment of programs	25. Management of discipline
20. Athlete eligibility	26. Ethical decision making
21. Safety and risk management	27. Fund raising

External relations	Internal relations
28. Media liaison	31. Rules compliance
29. Liaison with parents	32. Athlete eligibility
30. Liaison with other schools	33. Equitable distribution of resources

Personal performance characteristics
34. Development of effective working relationships
35. Professional conduct
36. Punctuality
37. Complete, accurate, and on-time paper work
38. Commitment

Step 2: Generate the Job Description

The job description is a written document that substantiates the expectations that the organization holds for the performance of the employee by outlining the specifics of what the job entails (Buford et al., 1988; Deets & Tyler, 1986; Grote, 1996; Murphy & Cleveland, 1991). It is a critical component of the evaluation because it defines performance in a clearly written form and because it is job-specific. It is important that the job description be concise and clearly worded, define the breadth and nature of the work, and outline the skill, responsibility, and complexity involved (Chelladurai, 1999). Examples of such job descriptions for a university coach and a high school athletic director are shown on pages 34-38.

Step 3: Define the Domain of Performance

The *domain of performance* contains all behaviors and tasks considered to be important contributors to job performance. It is a list of those indicators generated by the job analysis in step 1. Whereas the job analysis step is a field exercise of actually collecting data on what happens in a particular job, defining the domain of performance involves specific analysis of the list generated in step 1. Which of the tasks and behaviors observed through step 1 were deemed of specific importance to be further defined in step 2, the development of a written job description? How were they categorized in terms of importance? Which specific duties are defined repeatedly? Step 3 is meant to be an exercise of listing the specific items defined in step 1 and operationalized in step 2. Thus, the domain of performance provides specific indicators of evaluation criteria. It is devised by assessing the job

Job Description (last updated: 07/01/2001)

Position: *Head Women's Basketball Coach*

Department: *Department of Athletics, University of Westerbrooke*

Preamble

This position encompasses primary accountability for the direction of day-to-day activities and program development for University of Westerbrooke women's basketball. The incumbent is responsible for adhering to all department and league policies and procedures, and reports directly to the director of athletics.

This position is considered integral to the department as it seeks to fulfill the mission of providing university students opportunities for participation in highly organized competitive sport.

It is intended that coaches be guided by the following values that are endorsed by all department members and that define our desired organizational climate. Generally, these values include a commitment to the following principles:

1. The pursuit of professional and personal excellence
2. Information sharing
3. Fairness, honesty, and integrity
4. Gender equity within programming
5. The projection of a positive image at work and in the community
6. Academics-before-athletics approach for student-athletes
7. Priority given to the safety of all program participants
8. A coaching commitment to planning in order to maximize

   (a) direction,
   (b) motivation,
   (c) instruction,
   (d) progress information,
   (e) production,
   (f) positive experience,
   (g) sportsmanship,
   (h) variety,
   (i) self-determination,
   (j) social experience, and
   (k) support

These outcomes will be achieved through the following five categories of specific behaviors, tasks, activities, and responsibilities:

1. Day-to-day coaching
2. Recruiting

3. Athlete/team outcomes
4. Program administration
5. Public relations and professional development

Specific behaviors, tasks, activities, and responsibilities

The University of Westerbrooke women's basketball coach is responsible for the following:

1. The day-to-day application of coaching as it pertains to . . .

    a. Utilization of current and specific theory and techniques toward optimally training basketball athletes to reach their fullest potential

    b. Teaching appropriate basketball skills, game tactics, and strategies, while using effective techniques for skill and movement analysis

    c. Making appropriate coaching decisions during competition

    d. Developing a positive interpersonal relationship with athletes and student personnel involved with the program

    e. Developing specific practice and game plans

    f. Motivating, disciplining, and leading athletes toward their highest possible achievements

    g. Developing a positive, professional relationship with game officials, league personnel, and coaching colleagues

    h. Developing a disciplined team in both conduct and appearance, as judged both on and off the court

2. Building the basketball program through recruiting

    a. Establishing a recruiting plan for identifying, contacting, and communicating with top high school athletes in (a) the city and county area, (b) this and neighboring states, and (c) other areas of the country with reasonable potential for successful recruiting

    b. Bringing potential student-athletes to visit our campus to tour academic and athletic facilities, and to meet with both athletic and academic individuals

    c. Establishing a public relations link with scholastic- and club-level basketball both locally and state-wide, and if possible nationally, in order to increase the visibility of your program, yourself, and our university

    d. Working to achieve a basketball profile at all levels via media opportunities, attendance at games whenever possible,

(continued)

        volunteer coaching in club programs or clinics, and speaking engagements

    e. Working toward the recruitment goal: quality of athlete first, quantity of athletes second

3. Anticipated athlete and team outcomes

    a. Improvement over the course of a season, or from previous seasons assessed on a year-by-year basis

    b. Team and individual athlete accomplishments in relation to their potential

    c. Participation in the playoffs, or being in the top half of the league

    d. Satisfaction of team members

    e. Team cohesiveness

    f. Athlete-centered approach to coaching

4. Administrative tasks associated with coaching

    a. Being accountable for all financial matters related to travel, purchase of equipment, and the like

    b. Planning for both the short and long term, in relation to optimal preparation for the duties of the preseason, season, and postseason

    c. Attending league and national meetings

    d. Monitoring athlete eligibility and academic standing and progress

    e. Being on time with paper work

    f. Contributing to the overall atmosphere of the department through establishing positive team-oriented working relationships with peers

    g. Defining an effective competitive schedule within budget constraints

5. Public relations and professional development

    a. Aggressively pursuing the development of a relationship with local media

    b. Serving on department/university committees

    c. Conducting summer sports campus (where applicable)

    d. Being involved with professional association (where applicable)

e. Upgrading education, particularly coaching education, through achieving formal certification

f. Becoming and remaining a resource person for high school and elementary school coaches (where applicable)

g. Attaining Coaching Certification Course Conductor status and offering basketball certification courses in the local area

Sunnybrooke High School, Department of Physical Education

Job Description: *Athletic Director*   Accountable to: *High School Principal*

Job Purpose: Management of the SHS interscholastic sports program, with specific responsibility for organization, planning, evaluation, leadership, and internal and external relations

Manages: 20 varsity sport activities and associated coaching staff

Specific responsibilities:

1. Organization: the incumbent will have good overall knowledge of school sports and strong organizational skills. The incumbent will be responsible for organizing or supervising the coach's organization of all aspects of team travel; purchase of equipment; inventory and storage of equipment; the management of home games, including securing major and minor officials; and training and scheduling student workers. The incumbent will ensure that all aspects of the high school sports program comply with the standards set by the league of play and the rules governing the individual sport, especially as they pertain to student-athlete eligibility for competition.

2. Planning: the athletic director will ensure proper planning for all sports by outlining or supervising the planning of competitive schedules, practice schedules, facility scheduling, and the definition of equitable hosting parameters. The incumbent will also be responsible for planning budgets, staffing arrangements, the efficient use of personnel, and the development of common rules policy.

3. Evaluation: the athletic director will ensure the training, supervision, and appraisal of all staff; will evaluate or define a procedure for evaluating the overall sports program; will ensure compliance to rules of athlete eligibility; and will evaluate all programs, policies, facilities, and staff actions to ensure the safety of all participants and to strategically manage the inherent risk associated with sport.

(continued)

37

(continued)

4. Leadership: it is expected that the athletic director will provide overall leadership in all matters pertaining to the interscholastic sports program, and to ensure that common practices align with school philosophy. Such policy development should include, but not be limited to: equitable distribution of programming and resources for boys' and girls' sport; management of discipline in accordance with school policy; all matters related to fund raising; and the assurance of ethical decision making and support for an environment of fair play.

5. External and internal relations: the athletic director is expected to work with external partners such as parents, the media, officials from other schools, and the league within which the school's teams operate. The athletic director is also expected to manage the department internally to ensure proper communication, rules compliance, and the fair and equitable distribution of resources. The internal environment will be enhanced by the stellar professional conduct of the athletic director, and the athletic director's ability to develop effective working relationships, commitment, and management skills regarding efficiency.

description and listing all items considered to be components of success. This broad list may then have other appropriate yet tangential factors added that may not have been listed within the job description but are considered to be important determinants of successful performance. For example, a coach's job description may list items outlining procedures relative to practices: effective organization, frequency, teaching techniques, communication, and so on. However, it may be appropriate to add to the domain of performance a criterion that addresses behaviors associated with the philosophical orientation of the institution that should guide the coach's actions. In the university setting, this might involve the coach demonstrating support for the student-athletes' academic priorities when conflicts arise between attending practice and attending class. The same argument holds for the high school athletic director mentioned previously. These are examples of domain of performance items for the university coach:

Communicating with athletes	Making recruiting contacts
Adhering to budget	Making the playoffs
Performance improvements— individual and team	Receiving coaching awards
Performance improvements from previous year	Speaking engagements

Performance of individual athlete(s)	Applying sport knowledge
Motivating athletes to achievement	Utilizing game tactics and strategies
Adhering to rules and regulations	Teaching techniques during practice
Making decisions during competition	Conducting practice sessions
Complying with institution's philosophy	Developing game plans
Working relationships with department staff	Being on time with paper work
Caring for athlete's academic success	Developing effective coach-athlete relationships
Working relationships with peer coaches	Conducting summer sports camps
Monitoring athlete eligibility	Invited public appearances
Applying conditioning principles	Upgrading certification
Working with high school coaches	Team win-loss record
Planning and preparing for each seasonal phase	Scouting opponents
Establishing a recruiting plan	Maintaining and using statistics
Recruiting a specific number of athletes	Recruiting quality athletes
Writing for publication	Purchase of equipment
Involvement with professional association	Caring for the student-athlete's academic success
Enforcing discipline	

Examples of domain of performance items for a high school athletic director include the following:

Communicating with staff	Hiring quality staff
Adhering to budget	Appraisal of staff
Fund raising	Equitable decision making
Performance improvements from previous year	Speaking engagements
Development of policy	Applying sport knowledge

Motivating staff

Adhering to rules and regulations

Complying with school's philosophy

Working relationships with peers

Building competitive schedules

Invited public appearances

Upgrading certification

Team success rates

Supervision of staff

Contribution to league organization

Purchase of equipment

Working relationships with department staff

Professional conduct

Upgrading with professional development opportunities

Safety and risk management

Punctuality

Developing yearly plans

Hosting effective events

Monitoring athlete eligibility

Training of staff

Implementation of policy

Planning and preparing for each seasonal phase

Maintaining and using statistics

Writing for publication

Involvement with professional association

Being on time with paper work

Establishing working relationships with parents

In a nutshell, all behaviors or behavioral outcomes valued by the employer must be derived and formalized within the domain of performance.

Step 4: Ensure a Representation of Criteria Categories

As mentioned earlier, there are three main types of appraisal criteria:

1. Task-related behavioral process factors
2. Maintenance-related behavioral process factors
3. Behavioral product factors

Although the larger segment of the defined appraisal criteria emanating from the domain of performance should be exceedingly job-specific (i.e., should involve criteria that most closely reflect the main tasks of the job, or task-related process factors), it is also important that both outcomes of job behaviors and behaviors necessary to maintain the job environment be included in the inventory of appraisal criteria. Therefore, for the athletic team coach I recommend that a balance of the following sample criteria be assessed along with outcome measures such as win-loss record (product) or playoff participation (product):

- Expert application of conditioning principles (task-process)
- Decision making during competitions (task-process)
- Motivating athletes toward higher levels of achievement (task-process)
- Adhering to budget (maintenance-process)
- Working relationships with department staff (maintenance-process)
- Involvement with professional association (maintenance-process)

Likewise, the criteria used to evaluate the high school athletic administrator should include the three types of criteria, as in the following description:

- Managing the yearly budget without deficit (product)
- Hosting two city and one state championship per year (product)
- Ensuring that equipment is securely stored during the off-season (task-process)
- Defining fair practice schedules to effectively utilize facilities (task-process)
- Developing effective working relationships with league personnel (maintenance-process)
- Keeping on top of paper work to facilitate timely decisions (maintenance-process)

Step 5: Investigate the Impact of the Environment

To develop truly specific performance criteria, contextual factors in the environment must be investigated. This model describes a procedure for making evaluation criteria specific to the job in question. Two categories of the environment may affect the job: the external and internal environment. External environmental factors are those contextual issues outside the organization that may affect an individual's job performance within the organization. They usually include economic, social, legal, or political factors imposed on the organization from outside (Murphy & Cleveland, 1991). For example, public opinion regarding an institution may greatly affect the coach's ability to recruit student-athletes. If the social or political environment is negatively affecting the coach's recruiting, or differentially affecting one coach over another, consideration of environmental impact is necessary when appraising the coach's performance. I've found this to be the case when assessing the success of a coach's recruiting. The recruiting results of one swim coach appeared to be dismal. Yet, upon further investigation, this coach was severely disadvantaged because the top athletes came from feeder programs in larger centers with Olympic-sized training facilities. Unfortunately, our small institution located in a small town was not competitive in this setting. Many factors hampering the coach's recruiting were outside of his control. Similarly, a high school athletic administrator may be severely hampered in her ability to run a successful athletic program because of funding cuts to school extracurricular activities precipitated by a major economic recession. This may result in cuts to the school's programming, for which the administrator should not be held accountable because they are externally imposed.

Internal environmental factors are those contextual factors within the organization that may affect the performance of an employee or act to advantage one over another. The budget devoted to the coach's program is a case in point. A reduced or unequal travel budget among sports could drastically reduce exhibition travel. Assuming that exhibition games require travel and are critical to team preparation, this might result in reduced competitiveness. The coach of the team possessing the larger travel budget may be distinctly advantaged if the win-loss record is included in the evaluation criteria.

The athletic administrator may also face issues within an organization that fall outside his or her sphere of control. For example, if management of discipline is a criteria that the high school athletic director is accountable for, an overzealous vice principal who coincidentally lacks interest in sport and imposes an extensive sanction such as indefinite suspension against a team that misrepresents the school in some minor way should not necessarily be held accountable for such an action. These environmentally imposed factors must be considered when evaluating job performance. Both of these situations have the potential to influence the employee's ability to excel in the job and are therefore identified as possible influences within the process. Once detected, it is important to identify these factors for the situation at hand. Then, at appraisal time, the issues can be taken into account.

In summary, the preceding discussion proposed a model based on theory regarding the development of job-specific performance appraisal criteria. The discussion outlined a stepwise procedure for developing criteria and advocated the use of a balance of the end-product criteria classifications in the evaluation process.

Because lament for the lack of evaluation put into use for the assessment of athletic coaches has been a common topic in the sport management literature, and because this issue has been linked to the difficulty of developing job-specific performance criteria, we now turn our attention to developing criteria for evaluating athletic coaches. In an attempt to further operationalize the question of what criteria should be used to appraise university coaches in Canada, MacLean and Chelladurai (1995) developed the Scale of Coaching Performance. It is an excellent example of the development of performance appraisal criteria for a specific situation in the sport context.

The Scale of Coaching Performance

The Scale of Coaching Performance (SCP) evolves from the theory presented previously. It consists of six categories or dimensions of coaching performance, defining two dimensions for each of the main criteria types of behavioral products, task-related processes, and maintenance-related processes (see figure 2.2; for in-depth information on the development of the scale and its psychometric properties, please refer to MacLean & Chelladurai, 1995). The six dimensions defining the proposed model of coaching performance are operationally defined as follows:

1. *Team products:* outcomes of coaching that accrue only to the team or individual athletes forming the team.

2. *Personal products:* outcomes of coaching that accrue only to the coach.

3. *Direct task behaviors:* application of interpersonal skills and appropriate strategies and tactics used to enhance the performance of individual athletes and the team as a whole.

4. *Indirect task behaviors:* activities such as recruiting, scouting, and application of statistics that contribute indirectly to the success of the program.

5. *Administrative maintenance behaviors:* adherence to policies, procedures, and budget guidelines, and interpersonal relations with superiors and peers that strengthen the administration of the whole enterprise.

6. *Public relations maintenance behaviors:* liaison activities between one's program and relevant community and peer groups.

The individual criteria in each of the six dimensions resulted from the stepwise procedure described earlier where job assessment, job descriptions, and the resultant domain of performance were investigated for the position of Canadian university coach. The complete set of criteria contained in the SCP are listed in table 2.2.

Let us conclude this discussion on appraisal criteria with some comments on several other important issues that warrant consideration.

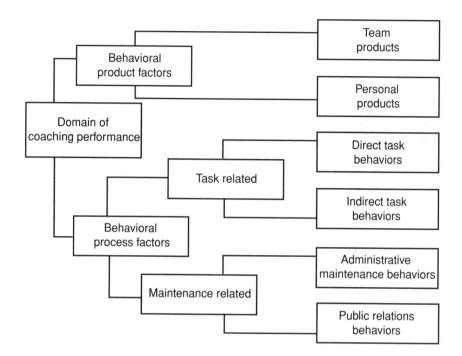

Figure 2.2 Theoretical model of dimensions of coaching performance.

Table 2.2 Coaching Performance Criteria Categories of the Scale of Coaching Performance

	Team products of coaching	Personal products of coaching
Behavioral product factors	Team win-loss record Making the playoffs Performance improvements—individual and team Performance improvements from previous year Performance of individual athlete(s)	Receiving coaching awards Writing for publication Invited public appearances Speaking engagements Upgrading certification
	Direct task process	**Indirect task process**
Behavioral process factors—task-related	Communicating with athletes Applying sport knowledge	Making recruiting contacts Scouting opponents

	Direct task process	Indirect task process
	Motivating athletes to achievement	Establishing a recruiting plan
	Utilizing game tactics and strategies	Maintaining and using statistics
	Applying conditioning principles	Recruiting a specific number of athletes
	Teaching techniques during practice	Recruiting quality athletes
	Making decisions during competitition	
	Conducting practice sessions	
	Planning and preparing for each seasonal phase	
	Developing game plans	
	Administrative maintenance processes	**Public relations maintenance processes**
Behavioral process factors— maintenance-related	Monitoring athlete eligibility	Working with high school coaches
	Adhering to budget	Conducting summer sports camps
	Adhering to rules and regulations	Establishing working relationships with parents
	Working relationships with department staff	Involvement with professional association
	Purchase of equipment	Presenting at player/ coaching clinics
	Being on time with paper work	
	Working relationships with peer coaches	
	Complying with institution's philosophy	

Other Issues Relative to Performance Appraisal Criteria

The intent of this chapter is to provide a discussion on issues relative to performance appraisal criteria. In order to meet this goal, a brief discussion on rating problems, criteria measurability, and links to training is presented in the following sections.

Rating Problems

Previously it was argued that the use of job-specific performance appraisal criteria is critical to effective evaluation. That being maintained, other issues concerning criteria can reduce the effectiveness of the evaluation by contributing to rating problems. Carroll and Schneier (1982) suggested that the most prevalent issues leading to rating problems involve criteria contamination, deficiency, and relevance.

In a nutshell, if criteria include aspects of behaviors that are not determinants of job success, they are considered contaminated. For example, a fitness instructor might be evaluated using the following criteria: ability to effectively teach fitness activities; use of voice; talent for encouraging participants; effective management of the class rosters; ability to vary class activities to prevent boredom; and willingness to gear activity closely to advertised content. To make the fitness instructor responsible for the organization's yearly profit margins would in effect contaminate the criteria for evaluating this specific position. Likewise, if certain important components of success are omitted, the criteria are said to be deficient. If our fitness instructor was evaluated only on his ability to vary class activities to prevent a lapse into monotony, he would not be accountable for several other important criteria of successful performance in the position, such as his use of effective teaching methodology and his ability to gear classes to the needs of the customer. In addition, criteria must accurately reflect the job under evaluation, meaning that they should be relevant to success for the particular position in question. That is, it is probably irrelevant that the fitness instructor is an excellent swimmer. Evaluating him for his success as a swimmer would result in a major error in rating.

Relevant criteria must also be valid and reliable. Validity refers to the degree to which the evaluation system actually measures what it says it is going to measure. Looking specifically at the individual criteria, two types of validity are important in assuring that the evaluation criteria measure what they are supposed to measure. These two types are termed *construct validity* and *content validity*. Construct validity refers to the extent to which an evaluation system actually measures the theoretical construct, such as the technical skill required to effectively coach a team. Mathematical formulae are used to determine scores of validity on a continuum. Content validity is a judgment regarding the degree to which items of evaluation actually reflect the content of the job. This is normally achieved by a panel of experts, for example all the coaches and athletic administrators within a college athletic department, who assess the data gathered in a job analysis. Finally, reliability is the degree to which different raters will come up with the same rating of performance. Although it is often estimated using statistical measures such as correlation coefficient, reliability is affected by rater knowledge. Thus, consistent methods of data collection among several raters on the performance of one individual, and also within one rater for assessing the performance of several different individuals, must be established (Bernardin, Alvarez, & Cranny, 1976).

In summary, it is important that every effort be made to ensure that rating problems be minimized. This can be attempted by understanding how to develop criteria that are free from contamination and deficiency, but are at the same time relevant to the successful completion of the job under scrutiny. When developing performance appraisal criteria, I've found it helpful to stop and assess each category for their relevance, and then to give some thought to reliability and validity by thinking about how performance will be measured against these criteria, and how data will be collected to measure such performance. Criteria must be both valid (measure what they purport to measure) and reliable (provide consistent measurements among different raters).

Criteria Measurability

Criteria measurability refers to the degree to which the individual criteria listed for evaluating a job can actually be measured. The issue of measurability is often discussed as a precursor to effective evaluations and is intricately linked to the issue of validity. However, defining a mechanism for ensuring that performance appraisal criteria actually are measurable is sometimes challenging. Many authors mention the issue in relation to developing construct validity (ensuring the criteria measure what they are supposed to), operationalizing constructs (precisely defining what is meant by a specific criterion), the potential for multidimensional criteria (criteria that have several different component parts), and leniency bias (giving favorable ratings because it's impossible to really know the true value of a criterion) (Fleishman & Mumford, 1991; Horn, 1992; Ivancevich & Glueck, 1989; Kane, Bernardin, Villanova, & Peyrefitte, 1995). Usually, methods of establishing measurability involve the use of operational definitions, content analyses, and statistical measures. The authors listed in this paragraph provide further information on the issue of measurability.

The measurability of the criteria espoused by the Scale of Coaching Performance have been considered (MacLean, 1997). Through content analysis, extensive library search, and construct evaluation, I concluded that measurability of the coach's success at both *communication* and *motivation* were most at issue. Let's investigate further the reasons why.

A look at social systems theory provided insight into the issue of communication. According to Montgomery and Fewer (1988) communication is dependent on context, mutual involvement of the actors, and environment.

Healthy communication has been operationalized as open and honest, involving active listening, a medium conducive to avoiding distractions, and a feedback–question answering phase (McKenna & Beech, 1995; Williams, 1998). Conversely, unhealthy communication is restricted, vague, ingratiating, dishonest, and indirect (Smilansky, 1997; Tompkins, 1997). The point to all of this is that a considerable number of factors contribute to the notion of communication, and that this criterion must be specifically defined or operationalized before it can be effectively measured. From my experience, appraising a coach or other instructor on communication is tricky unless you clearly define what communication is expected and how it will be measured. Otherwise, in the coach-athlete example, the athlete may suggest the coach was a very poor communicator because she didn't like the message being given. This, of course, is a different issue to be distinguished from poor communication, and a great example of why multidimensional criteria can present challenges within the performance appraisal process.

The same issue can be presented for the criterion of motivation that is also an individual measure of the Scale of Coaching Performance. I've found, and the research suggests, that in order to maximize the ability to motivate an individual, one must set clear objectives, minimize weaknesses, maximize strengths, be individualistic, link to goal setting, and use feedback and rewards (Horn, 1985; Locke & Latham, 1984; Orlick, 1980; Tompkins, 1997; Wriston, 1992). As an effective criterion for evaluation, "motivation" would therefore need to be specifically defined within the job description.

The other three criteria within the SCP that merit an investigation of measurability include decision making during competitions, interpersonal relationship skills (i.e., working relationships with peers and staff), and improvements of individual athletes' performances (depending on the nature of the sport). The point to all of this is that it is important to assess the measurability of individual criteria. Before using them in the system, it must be determined whether or not these criteria can be operationally defined. This can usually be accomplished, but it is not always easy or very obvious.

The Criteria-Training Dyad

It is also important to ensure that a link exists between the criteria defined for appraisal and the training that the job incumbent has received. Both items reflect directly on the human resource systems of the organization. In 1998, I completed a study (MacLean, 1998) to address this issue for the appraisal criteria espoused by the Scale of Coaching Performance and coach training in Canada, as evaluated by the National Coaching Certification Program (NCCP). The results of content analysis revealed an overall strong dyad between NCCP training and the items of the SCP. The main gaps in this particular training curriculum included items involved with recruiting and administrative tasks that one might rightly assume are specific to the job of university coach and would be covered in that setting. Again, the important point is that the criteria defined as being appropriate for use with the evaluation of a job must involve items that the job incumbent has been trained to accomplish. For example, imagine evaluating a strength training coach on her ability to dispense effective advice on nutrition.

Summary

This chapter emphasized the effects of the adage "Garbage in . . . garbage out!" The effectiveness of the performance appraisal system relies on the criteria used to evaluate. These criteria must be job-specific, relevant, comprehensive, valid, and measurable. Appraisal criteria that assess the behaviors associated with achieving the main tasks of the job and those maintaining the job environment are important for evaluation. In addition, criteria that reflect the outcomes of the behaviors important to the job are also a necessary component of the evaluation. The chapter also introduced a model outlining a procedure for defining job-specific performance criteria and operationalized this model with the development of the Scale of Coaching Performance.

Chapter 2 considered the *what* of performance appraisal systems. The purpose of the next chapter is to investigate the *how, who, when* and *where.*

IN THE MANAGER'S SHOES

The Facilities Services Coordinator

Reporting to the director, the facilities services coordinator is responsible for managing daily facility operations, such as set-up, internal bookings, and program requirements. He is also responsible for the supervision, assignment of job tasks, and the scheduling of overtime and vacation for five full-time equipment staff.

The facilities services coordinator is one of nine full-time staff responsible for operating the building and playing fields, seven days per week. There are eight tennis courts, six outdoor fields, a gymnasium, an indoor six-lane track facility, a pool, weight room facility, and dance studio.

Various kinds of events are hosted within the facility, from athletic tournaments and meets involving thousands of participants and spectators to individual fitness and open recreational play opportunities. The facilities services coordinator is responsible for both short and long term scheduling using computer software to enable on-line tracking of bookings from any terminal in the building. Events often require unique and detailed set-ups that the job incumbent must design, organize, and help deliver through the appropriate facility staff. Customer satisfaction is of paramount concern, and last-minute changes and minute details must be accommodated.

The facilities services coordinator is also responsible for the overall functioning of the equipment and infrastructure of the building. Overall building maintenance and the management of risk to ensure safety are important priorities. The job incumbent will conduct daily, weekly, or monthly checks of equipment as necessary. He will prepare and maintain detailed records of emergency situations, as well as a health and safety manual for all staff. When breakdowns or emergencies occur, he must be resourceful and able to invoke action planning based on the specific situation.

The facilities services coordinator is the immediate supervisor of five full-time individuals. He receives daily and weekly requests from the facility director and is accountable for guaranteeing that all work assignments are completed professionally and on time. Ensuring the communication of information in both directions within the organizational framework is vital to the smooth running of the operation. Vast amounts of information must be processed and prioritized weekly, and planning, training, and evaluating effectiveness are important considerations.

Specific accountabilities:

1. Schedules daily operational use.
2. Communicates repairs and required set-ups for events.
3. Supervises, trains, and schedules staff.
4. Performs duties of the director when she is unavailable.
5. Acts as first line of appeal in questions of dispute among facility users.
6. Acts as facility safety officer. Conducts daily, weekly, and monthly checks to ensure safety and the management of risk.
7. Designs new and more efficient layouts of the equipment dispensing areas and storage facilities to provide efficiencies and service.
8. Performs "on-call" duty for evenings and weekends when necessary.
9. Performs any other duties as required to ensure the smooth operation of the facility.

Use the model presented within this chapter to define job-specific performance appraisal criteria for the facilities services coordinator. The following questions should help to guide your answer:

Step 1: Complete a job assessment. Write a paragraph that summarizes a job assessment for the facilities services coordinator.

Step 2: Generate a job description. Using your answer from step 1, develop a job description by first listing the categories of the specific expectations for the job incumbent. Then develop the listings into a written job description document that lists the expectation for this specific position.

Step 3: Define the domain of performance. Break the functions listed in the job description into the three categories of performance appraisal criteria: behavioral product factors, behavioral process factors—task-related, behavioral process factors—maintenance-related.

Step 4: Ensure a representative balance of criteria types. Check to ensure that a reasonable balance exists for each category, and add anything that may have been missed (missed criteria usually relate to the maintenance of the job environment).

Step 5: Investigate the impact of the environment. Discuss whether the environment within which the facilities services coordinator works in this case would be a threat to the integrity of the criteria set for evaluating his or her performance. Which specific criteria might be most at risk of environmental influence?

Director of Marketing—Hawkley Golf & Country Club

The director of marketing position at Hawkley Golf & Country Club is an extensive job. The incumbent is responsible for marketing the entire operation directly as it relates to membership sales, special events and tournaments, and public relations. Michael Monroe has just been hired for this position. The job spans 12 months of the year, and unfortunately, excessive turnover of this position has been a problem for the club. Michael is the fourth person to hold this position in the last two years (see more about this in the chapter 5 case studies, pages 113-116).

The board of directors for Hawkley Golf & Country Club has drawn up the following job description for the position:

The director of marketing is responsible for

- market research, forecasting, and planning,
- soliciting, managing, and servicing sponsor partners,
- organization, pricing, and management of advertising,
- organization, pricing, and management of membership sales,

- development of all supporting and relevant promotional materials, and
- building of long-term relationships between the club and the business community.

The board of directors has also communicated to Michael that his job performance will be evaluated on the following criteria:

- Bottom line financial viability of the club
- Number of new members attracted each year
- Number of new sponsors attracted each year
- Perceptions of members of the board regarding the overall image of the club
- Advice of the club professional regarding the marketing director's overall performance

Do these criteria represent an effective means of assessing the job performance of the director of marketing? Why or why not, and if not, what criteria might be used to assess this position?

See appendix C for reflections on the cases.

THREE

Performance Appraisal Procedure: How, Who, When, and Where?

Up to this point this book has focused on the need to evaluate employees, as well as what should be appraised. Let's turn our attention now to the specifics of how to go about a performance appraisal. As presented earlier, several different tools or forms can be used in any chosen system. However, the forms do not make up the performance appraisal system. Rather, the term *system* denotes the need for an ongoing, active process that involves the gathering of information from multiple sources over time, the facilitation of communication and idea interchange, and the achievement of both personal and organizational goals. This may seem an overwhelming and time-consuming task, and indeed, these factors are often mentioned by managers in organizations that are not assessing employee performance regularly. However, performance appraisal need not be overwhelming, and it does not have to consume inordinate amounts of time. The most critical factor for successfully launching performance appraisal in your organization is the development of a *system*. Just as there are procedures for managing facilities, events, financial matters, and marketing initiatives, there also must be a procedure for appraising employee performance. Such a procedure or system should define what to do, how to go about it, when it should occur, and where it should take place. Once defined, it becomes another component of the job responsibility of the person(s) to whom it is assigned. Accordingly, this individual needs to be trained and given regular opportunities for upgrading skills. This chapter will provide the information needed to develop and implement a performance appraisal system, and will promote one particular performance appraisal system for use within sport organizations.

The Preliminary Stage: Getting Perspective

In the same way that evaluation criteria must be job-specific and that organization-specific contextual factors must be considered when defining criteria, the procedure developed for evaluating personnel is also situation-specific. When beginning to develop the system, you must discuss three main factors. First, the number of employees to be assessed must be considered. If, for instance, an organization has 500 employees to be assessed by one individual, then a time-consuming interview process is likely not manageable. Second, the complexity and design of the job in question will influence to some degree the development of the appraisal system. If considerable autonomy is associated with the job, then a highly structured, complex task rating process may not apply, whereas an open-ended essay format might be more appropriate. Third, and most important, the system must be closely tailored to employee and organizational needs and goals, and it must be practical. There is no definitive answer to choosing the best system. The utility and appropriateness of different procedures and methods of rating will change depending on situational determinants.

Although a simple rating system or checklist of achieved behaviors may be appropriate for one job, another may be best served by a system of goal setting as advocated with management by objectives (MBO). Once again, while arguing for situation-specific system development but realizing that every procedure will likely involve some method of appraisal followed by some means of communicating the resulting information, we will look specifically at MBO and make the case for this specific performance appraisal procedure for use in sport organizations.

How to Evaluate Sport Personnel: A Case for Management by Objectives (MBO)

MBO is a comprehensive philosophy of management put forth by Peter Drucker (1954) in his book *The Practice of Management.* Drucker argued for a harmonization of organizational and individual goals and called for heavier employee involvement in the setting of such goals. In its truest form, MBO is a system for planning, appraising performance, and defining organizational control. MBO is built on the premise of striving for open communication, mutual problem solving, and a positive organizational climate. It postulates a major emphasis on employee goal setting. Used as an appraisal technique, it is put into practice through the combination of goal setting, periodic reflection on successes achieved, and problem solving for improvement. For a detailed account of MBO procedures frequently used in appraisal, see Raia (1974) and Grote (1996). The following section introduces an adapted MBO process that I recommend specifically for evaluating personnel within a sport organization. Although it may appear to be a long, complicated process, MBO makes performance appraisal a year-round process of communicating and goal setting with employees. MBO actually links to many other managerial tasks, and will make your job of evaluating easier by focusing and communicating expectations via goals.

Designing the MBO Performance Appraisal System

The major steps proposed in the adapted MBO procedure include the following:

1. Ensure that the organizational mission as defined in the mission statement is up to date, openly communicated within the department, and reflective of the organization's climate.

2. Employ the model discussed in chapter 2 to define job-specific appraisal criteria for the position under evaluation, taking into consideration job analysis, the job description, and a mixture of process and product type criteria. Once completed, this stage of the process need only be revised if the job or job environment changes.

3. After circulation of the information produced in steps 1 and 2, schedule a *goals meeting* with the employee to ensure that there is agreement and understanding of the evaluation criteria, to define specific goals for the coming year, and to outline action plans for achieving such goals.

   Let's take a closer look at learning to effectively set goals. A goal is a specific end that one strives to achieve. An effective goal is one specific item that is concrete and challenging. Vague goals, such as "Do your best," are ineffective because of the inherent difficulty with measuring whether I've actually "done my best." The most effective goals, meaning those that both contribute to improving success and motivating the employee to want to achieve success, are (a) specific and (b) challenging, but (c) attainable (Locke & Latham, 1990). Some goals will be short-term, whereas others will be long-term. However, when possible, each goal should include a time limit for its achievement. Also, goals should include specific aspects of performance that are potentially within your area of control. They can be assigned and developed by both manager and employee, as recommended in this process. Goal statements emanate from the state of affairs of the organization and reflect your best thinking on items that will help either the employee or the organization, and thereby both of them, to be more effective at work.

4. Schedule a *progress meeting* at midpoint of the evaluation cycle to discuss progress and unforeseen factors that may impinge on goal achievement and, if necessary, to redefine goals.

5. Next, collate the performance data that has been periodically collected and solicit input from other appropriate sources (e.g., self, peer, subordinates).

6. Upon collation of all sources of input, hold a *year-end meeting* to communicate the findings and discuss the past year's performance, reinforce behaviors, motivate for continued success, and define goals for the coming year.

7. In a yearly performance review file keep a hard copy of all information discussed during this process. Both the supervisor and employee will sign the written appraisal.

8. This yearly cycle will then feed into a three-year cycle, in which a summary of these yearly appraisals is presented to the personnel committee for deliberation pertaining to global employment issues such as contract renewal. Recommendations are forwarded to the appropriate individual or group.

The University Volleyball Coach

To illustrate the procedure further, consider the following example of the university volleyball coach.

Step 1: Organization Mission It is unlikely that a university athletic department will not have a formal, written mission statement, but in the event that this occurs, a mission statement is a clear and concise statement that articulates purpose. The mission statement of one university athletic department states, "Our mission is to provide outstanding programs, services, and opportunities for participation in organized competitive sport for University XYZ's community. We are an innovative department committed to excellence and striving to make a positive impact on the quality of life and student experience." The specific references made to achieving such goals as excellence, outstanding programs, quality of life, and student experience should be noted and appear in some form within the appraisal process. For example, in the evaluation of the head coach for volleyball, one line reads, "Provides guidance to student-athletes regarding academic goals and time management skills." This criterion is an indicator of the coach's role in contributing to the athlete's quality of life and student experience. There should be many other obvious ties between the performance appraisal criteria and the organizational mission.

Step 2: Generation of Job-Specific Appraisal Criteria Using the model and procedure outlined in chapter 2, develop a list of appraisal criteria reflecting the behaviors associated with completing the job, the results of these behaviors, and factors relative to maintaining the work environment. Ensure that all contributions that are valued by the organization are noted and encouraged. For example, in the case of the university volleyball coach, the job description might encourage the employee to contribute to an organizational environment characterized by teamwork and the successful interaction of several employees. This contribution to the maintenance of the work environment can be assessed by criteria such as the incumbent's "attendance and contribution to discussions in weekly meetings," and "willingness to accept a fair share of the workload for hosting special events."

Step 3: Schedule Meeting #1—Goals Definition The goals definition meeting should take place in a private meeting room, and for the example of the university coach, it makes sense to hold it during May or June. This time marks the natural end of an academic year, and perhaps more importantly, the beginning of a new one. Notes should be taken to record the content of the meeting. Both the athletic director and coach should come to the meeting having considered where the priorities should lie for the coming year.

First, the participants in the meeting should agree on the evaluation criteria. It is important that the evaluation criteria used in the evaluation be very clear and that they be understood by everyone involved. Then, based on the discussion of the coach's achievement with these criteria, a discussion on future goals should take place. The goals defined must be prioritized. It is important to give priority weighting to specific goals so that the chosen areas of emphasis help to link the past to the future. Chosen priorities are based on what has occurred in the past, what can be improved, and what directions the coach wishes to pursue in the future. They are specific to this particular coach and her situation, and they serve to feed the establishment of specific goals that will define an emphasis of priorities for the coming year.

It may be that the coach in our example wishes to give precedence to some specific items that she feels require immediate focus. For instance, this coach may have fallen behind in the completion of coaching certification modules begun within the last three years, and these modules need priority status to ensure that they will be completed by a certain date. She may designate the specific criteria of "communicating to athletes" as one that repeatedly falls short of her expectation on Athlete Rating of Coach evaluation forms, and therefore might mark it for improvement. She may also foresee a large turnover of veteran athletes over the next two years, and thus might request that athlete recruitment be weighted more heavily.

As shown in the example, two things have been accomplished during the goals meeting. In discussing the importance of various criteria, the lines of communication have been opened. Second, goals for the coming season have begun to emerge. The goals need to be realistic, and depending on the complexity and nature of the specific goals, there are usually no more than three or four of them. It is also possible that a particular situation warrants one specific goal, such as the completion of a master's degree that has been in progress for five years. Once the specific goals are established, the participants should discuss how best to achieve the goal, and write a realistic action plan. It may be that the coach in this example has three uncompleted level IV coaching certification modules to finish, which in each case will require some reading and a written assignment for completion. It may be determined that the best course of action is for this coach to stay home and work on this project every Wednesday morning because time and distractions in the office are a hindrance to completion. The action plan required for improving communication to athletes might include selected reading in the coaching and psychology literature and attendance at a professional development workshop designed for business leaders that teaches the development of communication skills. This action plan may emphasize undertaking this activity in summer and early fall to ensure that ideas gathered through the training phase can be implemented with this year's team. Finally, the action plan for recruiting might incorporate prior athlete identification, a specific plan of events and tournaments to attend, a recruitment network of people to assist the process, and a schedule of plans related to contacts, campus visits, home visits, and "deal breakers" (phone call from the university president; name in lights on campus sign during visit; alumni and player testimonials; etc.). The end result is a written document that defines specific goals for the coming year, accompanied by an action plan that defines how to succeed in achieving them.

Step 4: Schedule Meeting #2—Progress Check-Up The progress meeting is usually very brief; for the coach in this example, it should occur in December. December marks the midpoint of the academic year and is a natural downtime for coaches as students write exams. The purpose of this meeting is to simply ask the questions, "How's it going?" and "Where are you in achieving the goals defined last summer?" The progress discussion is important because it serves as a reminder, as a motivator, and as an opportunity to redefine any goals that have become unrealistic as a result of unforeseen circumstances. This redefinition should not be confused with providing the coach with an escape from achievement. In other words, "I didn't get around to it" is not an acceptable excuse. However, it's important to remember that sometimes extenuating circumstances prevent the achievement of goals. For instance, after a coach searches and registers for a communications-based professional development seminar, the course may be canceled at the last minute because not enough people registered. This is certainly not the coach's fault, and an alternative method of achieving information on this topic should be sought.

At the least, this brief meeting serves as a reminder to the coach of her responsibility for specific achievement. The athletic director is able to help "coach" the coach.

Step 5: Collection of Performance Data In our example, the athletic director will continually gather information on the achievements of the coach. The director will take notes about incidents and observations of performance based on interactions, observations, and outside input. The coach will be observed during practices and games, and practice plans and other written documentation such as game plans and scouting files may be examined. The athletic director will ensure that first-hand information is observed or investigated for each of the performance criteria dimensions generated in step 2. This information may be documented using a rating scale format and by open-ended essays, as illustrated in "Performance Appraisal Notes: Head Coach" (pages 60-61). At the same time, the athletic director should collect and collate other sources of input pertaining to the coach's performance. It is recommended that several sources of input be collected, to include a Self-Evaluation form, a Peer Evaluation form, and a Student-Athlete Rating of Coaching form. Sample forms for each of these are presented in appendix B, sample forms B.7 through B.9. When rating scales are used, averages should be computed for each item along with an overall value. In addition, critical incidents and narrative points illustrating positive and negative performance should be pulled from the data and be included in the overall appraisal. Specific sources of input must remain anonymous. These data, along with the athletic director's evaluation, are summarized into a document for discussion at the year-end meeting.

Performance Appraisal Notes: Head Coach

Name: _Cindy Meehan_   Date: _November 13, 2001_

Setting: _Volleyball practice—mid-week, during competitive schedule_

Rating Scale Key: 5=Superior   4=Above average   3=Average
2=Below average   1=Inferior   0=Not applicable

Sport knowledge	0 1 2 3 ④ 5
Organization	0 1 2 ③ 4 5
Communication	0 1 ② 3 4 5
Planning	0 1 2 ③ 4 5
Motivation	0 1 2 ③ 4 5
Public speaking	0 1 ② 3 4 5
Teaching technique	0 1 2 ③ 4 5
Use of time	0 1 2 3 ④ 5
Athlete progression	0 1 2 ③ 4 5
Preparedness	0 1 2 3 ④ 5
Coaching decisions	0 1 2 3 ④ 5
Timeliness	0 1 2 ③ 4 5
Game planning	⓪ 1 2 3 4 5
Philosophy	0 1 2 ③ 4 5
Management ability	0 1 2 ③ 4 5
Effectiveness	0 1 2 ③ 4 5

Comments:

- Ratings made in comparison to peers at this level.
- Definitely need to discuss with Cindy a strategy for improved public speaking and communication with her athletes.
- Needs to improve clarity of verbal instructions: Speaks too quickly and never reiterates her point; in middle blocker drill she quickly made her point before having four athletes complete the drill. They clearly missed her instruction on lateral movement.

Overall Observations:

- Appears to know the game very well, needs help learning to impart her knowledge.

- Teaching techniques will likely improve with work on improved public speaking, communication skills.
- Very well organized; effective practice planning; good use of time. Perhaps a sense of too much urgency?
- Coaching decisions on player personnel seem effective, obvious to me.
- Well prepared and running an effective program for college level volleyball.
- Seems to be well respected by athletes.
- Might inquire about use of assistant coaches (check next time). Not sure of their role; seemed to be nothing specific for them to do.
- Check for more position-specific group work in future.

Step 6: Schedule Meeting #3—Year End: Looking Back and Looking Forward This meeting is a replica of the goals meeting described in step 3. It is not intended to be overly formal or acrimonious in any way. Rather, the participants should look back at how the athletic director, the athletes, the assistant coaches, and the coach herself viewed the year. It is an opportunity to discuss the accomplishment of the specific goals set at the same time last year. It is a performance management opportunity for the supervisor to applaud positives, discuss problems, reinforce the department's mission, and provide motivation for the pursuit of future goals. It is also the ideal time to set specific goals for the coming year.

Step 7: File Yearly Performance Review The information collected, and the discussion about it, is written up and signed by the athletic director and coach. This file then becomes a confidential and formal component of the organization's employment history.

Step 8: Three-Year Performance Appraisal Cycle The final component of this system involves integrating the yearly process into a longer appraisal cycle that is committee-driven (usually an organization's personnel committee) and that provides information to management about global employment issues. Such summative issues might include renewal, remuneration if it is not governed by a collective agreement process, length of contract, and rank. The athletic director is then in a strong position to present information and data from several sources collected over the three-year cycle to the personnel committee in order to fuel the discussion of more summative (bottom-line) employment issues. The resulting recommendation—which has been examined by several people, is made up of information from a variety of sources, and covers a reasonable period of time (2-5 years)—should then be forwarded to the appropriate body (such as the university committee on promotion) or person (such as the university president).

Business Manager, National Amateur Baseball Association

Let's consider another example of designing an MBO performance appraisal system, this time for a business manager of the National Amateur Baseball Association.

Step 1: Organization Mission The mission of the National Amateur Baseball Association is "to foster, encourage and develop the game of baseball, to service baseball programs in order to make the sport a readily accessible competitive or recreational option for all, regardless of sex, age, race or religion, and to stage first class competitive events on the National stage." As a first step in the evaluation of the business manager position, the current mission of the organization is assessed to gain an understanding of how the position fits into the larger goals of the organization. It's clear that the job description for this position must reflect management and financial planning direction for the overall goals of the organization, and that a major role of the job incumbent is support for administrative leaders. This is reflected in the position job description by items such as, "Maintain current spread sheets on all budget cost centers" and "Advise senior administrators on all matters of financial management." As a first step, an overall understanding must be gained regarding the scope of the job and its fit into the global objectives of the organization.

Step 2: Generation of Job-Specific Appraisal Criteria As described in the previous example, the model and procedure presented in chapter 2 for defining job-specific performance appraisal criteria is engaged. Job assessment and the defined job description provide the content of the *domain of performance*. Categories of process factors that are task- and maintenance-related, along with product factors, are defined, and in consideration of both the internal and external environment, evaluation criteria for the position are defined. In the case of the sport organization business manager, criteria such as "efficient financial record keeping" (task-process factor), "use of current computer technology" (maintenance-process factor), and "meets accounts payable schedule deadlines" (product factor) are relevant.

Step 3: Schedule Meeting #1—Goals Definition It makes sense to schedule the goals definition meeting for the business manager at the natural end of one fiscal year, which of course translates into the beginning of a new fiscal year. Given that year-end for the National Amateur Baseball Association is

March 31, it's appropriate to schedule the goals definition meeting during the month of April. At that time, both the business manager and director of the organization will come into the process, having considered where the priorities should lie for the coming year.

It is important that an open discussion on the criteria for evaluation ensue, and that both parties are well aware of the general criteria that are employed for evaluating the business manager. Next, several specific goals to be accomplished in the coming year should be discussed. The first priority might be the need to learn and implement a new computer software application program for check requisitioning. The second priority might involve a new system of deadlines for communicating important financial information to department managers. The third goal might relate to the director's concern that in the past several years the organization has not been able to accurately forecast membership numbers, and to the obvious problems for budgeting revenues presented by this issue.

A discussion for defining an action plan should come next. Such discussion is critical because it will enable the development of the best strategy for achieving the specific goals listed previously. For the first priority, the business manager might determine a procedure and time line for selecting and testing computer software for check requisitioning. For the second goal, ideas about the exact financial information important to individual department managers could be generated, and a course could be charted for collecting information from the constituents and implementing change. For the third goal, the participants might generate a plan for learning more about methods to forecast memberships, with care given to defining the steps and time lines for achieving this goal.

The business manager will leave the meeting with a clear understanding of the criteria used in his job performance evaluation. He will also have a clear understanding, in writing, of specific goals to accomplish next year, along with ideas and time lines for accomplishment.

Step 4: Schedule Meeting #2—Progress Check-Up The business manager and director should meet briefly in September (roughly halfway through the fiscal year) to discuss how the manager is progressing with the goals set during the goals definition meeting. This second meeting is usually very brief, but it is very important. It is an opportunity to discuss roadblocks to goal acquisition, and if necessary to redefine a goal that might have been impossible to achieve or that might have been overly ambitious. It also reminds the business manager of the importance of setting and achieving strategic goals, and to motivate him toward further accomplishment. For example, suppose the business manager left the goals meeting with every intention of achieving all three goals but spent all of his time working on the issue of forecasting membership numbers. In this case, the check-up meeting can help the business manager redirect some of his attention to the other two goals by delegating several tasks associated with membership forecasting to his staff. A course of action and time lines can thus be redefined.

Step 5: Collection of Performance Data The executive director of the National Amateur Baseball Association is charged with gathering information to evaluate the performance of the Association's business manager. The director takes notes on what, and how well, the manager is doing. The data collection phase includes notes regarding incidents and observations of performance based on interactions, observations, and relevant outside input. The settings for data collection include all on-the-job conditions within the office, in meetings, and in the field. Content analysis of completed work plays a large role in the data collection on this type of position. The director ensures that first-hand information is observed or investigated for each of the performance criteria dimensions generated in step 2. An example of a data collection instrument that might facilitate note taking is completed for this example in "Performance Appraisal Notes: Manager" (pages 65-66). Several of these forms will be completed and filed through the year as information relative to the incumbent's job performance becomes available. A peer and self-evaluation may also be used. Each source is then included in the overall performance evaluation, which is based on the criteria of performance as well as the goals set and agreed to at the beginning of the year. The evaluation document produced in this performance evaluation becomes one of the bases for discussion at the year-end meeting.

Step 6: Schedule Meeting #3—Year End: Looking Back and Looking Forward The year-end meeting is a replica of the goals meeting. Performance achievement is discussed by the director and business manager over the evaluation time period as it applies to accomplishment of the criteria and goals that were previously agreed on as important for success in this position. This is a time for the supervisor to commend positives, discuss problems, and reinforce the department's mission. This meeting also serves as the first step in setting goals for the coming year.

Step 7: File Yearly Performance Review The evaluation accomplished in step 6 is then produced in writing and signed off by both the director and business manager. This documentation then becomes a formal component of the confidential employment history of the employee during his tenure with this particular organization.

Performance Appraisal Notes: Manager

Name: _Timothy Howitt_   Date: _August 21, 2001_

Position: _Business Manager_   Time: _Previous two weeks_

Setting: _Check requisition computer software implementation process_

Rating Scale Key: **5=Excellent**   **4=Good**   **3=Average**
                     2=Below average   **1=Unacceptable**   **0=Not applicable**

Leadership	0 1 2 3 ④ 5
Organization	0 1 2 ③ 4 5
Communication	0 1 2 3 4 ⑤
Planning	0 1 2 3 ④ 5
Motivation	0 1 2 3 4 ⑤
Public speaking	0 1 2 3 4 ⑤
Personnel management	0 1 2 ③ 4 5
Use of time	0 1 2 ③ 4 5
Paper work	0 1 ② 3 4 5
Preparedness	0 1 2 ③ 4 5
Strategic planning	0 1 2 3 ④ 5
Timeliness	0 1 2 3 ④ 5
Event planning	⓪ 1 2 3 4 5
Philosophy	⓪ 1 2 3 4 5
Overall contribution	0 1 2 3 ④ 5
Effectiveness	0 1 2 3 ④ 5

Other:

Distribution of workload	0 1 2 3 ④ 5 _____	0 1 2 3 4 5
Technical understanding	0 1 2 3 ④ 5 _____	0 1 2 3 4 5
Handling input/advice	0 1 ② 3 4 5 _____	0 1 2 3 4 5
_____	0 1 2 3 4 5 _____	0 1 2 3 4 5
_____	0 1 2 3 4 5 _____	0 1 2 3 4 5
_____	0 1 2 3 4 5 _____	0 1 2 3 4 5

(continued)

(continued)

Comments:

- Really effective use of personnel implementing the new system—great seminar to communicate what, why, and how.
- Forgot to file paper work for warranty registration, but handled this effectively when reminded.
- Very solid planning of the project.

Overall Observations:

- Overall, job well done!
- Must be careful of ability to handle questions and queries, especially constructive criticism. Managed Mike's questions better than the area that Marcia brought up regarding backup system in the event of computer bugs, etc. Go over this example with him. No need to pursue until year-end unless provoked by other issues.

Step 8: Three-Year Performance Appraisal Cycle As described in the previous example, the final step incorporates the yearly appraisal into a longer evaluation cycle that matches a three- to five-year employment contract. The business manager may hold a three-year contract with the organization. In such a case it might be appropriate to have yearly performance reviews funnel to a performance appraisal committee of senior managers. The role of the committee then becomes multifaceted and will control global perspective for the organization regarding renewal of contracts, promotions, remuneration, and other human resource management issues. Depending on the size of the organization, the role of the committee may be held by one individual. Wherever possible, however, it is recommended that a committee of three to four senior managers be involved in making such important, summative decisions. Recommendations can be forwarded to the organization's board of directors or president for final authorization.

A Comment on the Practicality of the MBO System

As shown in the preceding examples, eight steps are recommended in the MBO system of performance appraisal for evaluating sport organization personnel. Busy sport managers may be thinking, "Just a minute here. There's no way I have time to complete all of these steps . . . forget it, I can't possibly make this a high enough priority to do all of that!" Time is an important consideration and an acknowledged concern. But consider this: First of all, the system as defined may have eight steps, but several of those need be accomplished only once for all of the employees you evaluate, and they may already be complete. For instance, it is likely that the organization already has a stated mission, which will expedite step 1. If this is not the case, the importance of having a mission statement and communicating it fully within the organization for purposes other than performance evaluation make its development worthy of the time and effort. It needs to happen anyway. For step 2, any evaluation system must include specific performance appraisal criteria for the job in question, but once these criteria are established, time is saved during subsequent evaluations. Evaluating the job based on criteria that are directly connected to job success (step 2) and collecting data from several sources representative of actual job performance (step 5) is mandated by employment law. This leads to the second important reason for making time to complete the steps outlined in the MBO procedure: Sport organizations simply cannot afford to deal with the disastrous legal and public relations ramifications that will result from doing evaluations ineffectively, haphazardly, or not at all. In many wrongful dismissal lawsuits, a paper trail of supportive evaluations contradicts the dismissal and provides grounds for the lawsuit. Still other lawsuits warn against conducting performance appraisals that are incongruent with promotions and rewards. Lawsuits are draining both financially and emotionally, and provide plenty of incentive to manage personnel through an effective system. In addition, the unpleasant necessity of retaining employees who successfully litigate against the organization is hugely counterproductive to maintaining a healthy, productive organizational culture. For all these reasons, having an effective system of evaluation is worth the time and trouble, and it's not as time consuming or difficult as it might seem. In fact, it's very rewarding to help individuals set and achieve goals.

Optimizing the Performance Appraisal System

Regardless of whether you are revising a current evaluation procedure or starting from scratch to develop a new one, the following points will help to ensure that you optimize the system to achieve the best possible results.

- Spend sufficient time to ensure you have developed criteria that are relevant to the job, important to organizational success, acceptable to the appraisee, and balanced with regard to behaviors and results.
- Make performance appraisal an ongoing process, as opposed to a finite task that must be endured once per year.
- Ensure that the nature and purpose of the appraisal system are well communicated within the organization.
- Use several sources of input for the appraisal, and strongly consider using some form of self-assessment to maximize open, two-way communication.

- Train the appraisers, and ensure that the appraisees are aware of this training.

- Give meaning to the system by ensuring that members of upper levels of management are committed to it, as demonstrated by actions (such as promotions or pay increases) that precipitate from appraisal trends.

Gaining Support for the Performance Appraisal System

The performance appraisal system will only be effective if the members of the organization believe in it and are committed to it. To achieve support for an ongoing, somewhat time-consuming, and sometimes distasteful set of tasks, it is imperative that the organization achieve and consistently reinforce the following three points.

First, communicate. Awareness of the evaluation process among employees is key to making them comfortable with the process and ultimately to gaining their support for the evaluation system. The easiest way to achieve acceptance is to talk about the process often, gather and incorporate opinions from those who will be evaluated, and make the process an everyday part of organizational life. A strategy of meetings and memos and the circulation of information, along with any other suitable methods of communicating, is necessary for encouraging support and ultimate success.

Second, the importance, utility, and ultimate results of the appraisal system must be personalized. The people being evaluated must be able to see how their efforts contribute to the organization's goals, as well as to their own personal goals. This awareness of how they fit into a larger plan can be both motivational and empowering. The focus of such discussions is not, "You need to do your job better," but rather, "You play a critical role in helping this organization. By moving toward the achievement of your own goals, you are helping us all move closer to achieving overall organizational goals." To gain the support of senior management, the link between organizational and employee achievement of goals must be highlighted. And finally, those performing the appraisal will need to see that performance appraisal actually facilitates their communication with subordinates and enables them to help employees achieve their goals at work.

Third, the performance appraisal system must contribute to organizational action in order for employees to support it. A system that always produces favorable feedback regardless of performance, that does not distinguish between poor and good performance, or that results in the same levels of support for all employees (remuneration, promotion, etc.) is likely to simply be ignored.

Implementing the Performance Appraisal System

Whether implementing a newly created system or revising an old one, it is best to create an implementation team that includes individuals from all areas of the organization or department. Ideally, these individuals will be supporters of regular performance appraisal and have credibility among their peers. The implementation team must thoroughly understand and receive training in the system being launched. After this training, the purpose of the implementation team is to communicate information about what the system entails to their assigned areas. The goal of this process is to develop appreciation and acceptance of the system throughout the organization. For a very small organization (five or six individuals) this may include a committee of the whole. In other organizations, which might be compartmentalized into departments, perhaps one or two individuals from each department might belong to the committee. These individuals can be those who have previously been designated for having responsibility for implementing the evaluation process (normally, the department managers). It might also be appropriate to allow each department to nominate and elect one or two individuals for the committee, based on their interest, job functions, and work load.

The group should be trained by the leader responsible for directing performance appraisal in the organization. If necessary, an outside consultant could be hired to perform such training. Further details about training are presented in chapter 5.

Collecting Performance Appraisal Data

The performance appraisal system must define procedures for data collection. The information gathered and used to assess the performance of an individual must obviously link back to the criteria defined as important to the position. The process of data collection needs to be ongoing in order to formulate a file for an individual. The information in the file could include notes written from supervisor observations, input from others, and content analysis of written work. The file is ultimately a running account of how that individual is proceeding with job tasks and goals.

Once again, using the example of the university athletic coach, we would expect the athletic director to schedule unobtrusive visits to practices, games, and team meetings to observe the coach in action. Making only one observation can be dangerous because it can leave the evaluator with an entirely unrepresentative impression of the coach's performance. Thus, one should conduct six to ten observations of the coach while the coach is working over the course of the season. The observer should take notes and solicit input from assistant coaches' criteria items. Practice and training plans can be reviewed periodically.

Most importantly, a strategy that defines the content and timing of data collection is a necessary component of the performance appraisal system. A well-defined procedure, carried out when evaluating all employees, contributes to consistency within the system. Collecting information over the course of the evaluation period will also enable timely feedback. Some performance issues may need to be addressed immediately, as opposed to waiting for the year-end appraisal meeting. In some cases, the timely relay of feedback from specific incidents makes all the difference in improving both individual and organizational performance.

Consider the athletic trainer working in a national training center. The trainer's supervisor would be expected to schedule visits to the clinic to observe the employee in action. Several "drop-in" visits should be scheduled over the course of the evaluation period. The visits should be documented. Other critical incidents, both positive and negative, that illustrate the job incumbent's performance should also be documented as they occur. The observer could assess the content of training manuals and gather input from peer and self-assessments. One of the most important sources of input to the evaluation might come from the athletes the trainer works with on a regular basis. In this case, the athletes must have a mechanism for providing feedback on the trainer's performance. An example of a questionnaire for collecting such input is provided in appendix B.

The importance of collecting accurate, representative, factual information that can be documented as the basis for the performance assessment cannot be overemphasized. With the preceding information detailing how to go about developing an evaluation system, and with specific reference to developing an MBO goal-setting-based system in sport organizations, let us move forward to discuss who should be involved in the process.

Who Should Be Involved in Performance Appraisal?

Clearly, the responsibility for conducting the performance appraisal must rest with the immediate supervisor of the employee. In some situations, the immediate supervisor may provide input to the next level of supervisor who has the ultimate responsibility for evaluation. However, it is recommended that the managers most closely and directly responsible for supervising an employee be assigned the task of performance appraisal.

For example, personnel in a college or university athletic department would be evaluated by the athletic director. Departmentalized sport organizations such as an Olympic association might have project leaders who would feed information on performance to group project leaders for ultimate appraisal. Most importantly, an individual who is several organizational levels removed from the employee, and who thus is rarely in a position to know specifically of the employee's performance, must not hold this responsibility. Of course, the reverse problem might occur if an individual too closely associated with or involved in the employee's work completed the assessment, resulting in an unfair or biased appraisal. For this reason, heavy emphasis should be placed on training the appraisers to issues of errors in rating. Another deterrent to bias is contained in the MBO procedure, which feeds information from yearly appraisals to a committee every three years. The committee will serve to safeguard the process, preventing the consolidation of power with one supervisor, while looking for trends in performance over several years.

The other important component of the "who" element of performance appraisal involves sources of input. The supervisor can observe the employee working and investigate the content of things the employee produces, or the outcomes of the employee's actions, but it is also critical that other points of view be collected. Given that a complete population survey that involves monitoring everything an employee does is not very feasible, the manager's goal is to collect a representative sample of information in order to paint an overall picture of the employee's performance. This sample must be inclusive and extensive enough to identify trends of strengths and weaknesses. The best method of validating such trends involves collecting information from multiple sources. Thus, it is proposed that several sources of input feed the performance appraisal system, and that self-evaluation also be used in order to maximize communication and block problems of misperception. This is commonly known today as the concept of *360-degree feedback* and is discussed thoroughly by a team of authors in the book *Maximizing the Value of 360-Degree Feedback* (1998), edited by Walter Tornow and Manuel London.

In simplistic terms, 360-degree feedback is a system in which performance is rated by a range of coworkers such as supervisors, peers, subordinates, and customers, and then compared to self-ratings of the job incumbent. From this set of information, a series of goals and the means for accomplishing these goals is derived. In the sport organization example, 360-degree feedback makes perfect sense, and performance assessment information should be collected from several different sources. Consider the example of a fitness instructor working at a fitness and health club. Data on the performance of the instructor can come from more than just the manager of the club. The perceptions of class participants, peer instructors, and the instructor's self-rating of performance on standardized criteria items can help to complete the picture of performance. Similarly, in the example of the college coach, it is recommended that in addition to the athletic director's appraisal, pertinent information also be collected from assistant coaches, athletes, support staff, and the coach's self-assessments. In these examples, such data would be collated by the club manager and athletic director, and depending on the method of data collection, averages of ratings or excerpts of narrative summations would feed the formal assessment. Those who provide information on the employee being assessed must be assured that they will remain anonymous. The end result will include a more representative picture of how well the employee has performed.

When Should Performance Appraisal Happen?

The short answer to the question of "When?" is "Throughout the year." As discussed previously, the process, to be effective, must be continual. However, formal evaluation meetings can be set for certain times of the year. The year-end meeting has already been discussed. At the season's end, the athletic coach does not have the daily pressures of training and competition preparation. At the natural year-end for the sport organization, a business manager is naturally wiping an old slate clean. Thus in each case, the employee has the time and relatively relaxed state of mind to address such issues as long-term planning and performance appraisal. Some organizations might not have a logical end-of-year time period. In such cases, the time set for the performance appraisal should be determined by the administrators involved, in accordance with the type of business conducted by the organization.

Beyond setting the year-end meeting, "How often?" is a question that needs to be addressed. Let us examine the MBO system detailed earlier in this chapter. The system is a continuing procedure of evaluation that includes employee goal setting with the express purpose of providing the employee with direction and assistance toward achieving yearly goals. It makes sense, then, that the appraisal procedure incorporates a yearly cycle of goal setting and biannual check-up meetings. The yearly cycle is manageable and for the sport organization employee reflects a normal season of activity. Postponing appraisal beyond one year negates the "coaching" function of the supervisor and can lead to a lack of focus in the employee. An annual cycle of appraisal is essential for maintaining strong communication and motivation toward goals. Normally, with formative evaluation in which the purpose of assessment is to provide constructive feedback and motivation toward achieving goals, a yearly cycle of performance assessment is advocated.

When the goal is summative in nature, with promotions and contract extensions in mind, however, a three- to five-year cycle is often incorporated. The three-year time frame proves an adequate but not too extensive time period. It also makes sense in that employment contracts often parallel this three-year duration. Conversely, setting employment contracts on a yearly basis, and looking at promotions and other rewards in this shorter time frame, is usually considered burdensome for everyone involved.

Optimally, data should be collected several times over the year. For example, an athletic director would need to observe a coach in action six to ten times in games and practices over the course of the season. It is recognized, however, that situations differ and that the recommendations for the performance appraisal of a coach might be very different in another situation.

Where Should Performance Appraisal Happen?

At first glance, "Where?" might appear to be a moot question. However, it is an important consideration. My research into evaluation for coaches has revealed that performance appraisal in sport organizations often occurs at the competition site. The coach's supervisor watches the competition, and, after the competition, stops by to say "Good job," or to make other comments. Informal appraisal, in this setting, ought not to be dismissed as unnecessary or undesirable, because it is essential that the coach receive support and feedback at these critical times, in action in the sport setting. Brief conversations at practice sites are also essential components of effective personnel evaluation in the sports realm. Of course, formal meetings should take place in professional, private office settings where interruptions are not tolerated.

Developing Good Interpersonal Skills

Communicating clearly is the most important aspect of the entire performance appraisal process. It is essential to look at the interpersonal and interview skills that will augment communication and maximize the effectiveness of the discussion.

It is very important that the manager be well prepared for any appraisal interview or discussion. Developing an outline of items to be covered and having documentation (such as appraisal forms, self-appraisals, actual work materials, and goal planning documentation) that will support the discussion is critical toward achieving focus and creating a factual, efficient, and meaningful exchange of ideas. The actual interview can be conducted in many ways, and personal style should help to guide the process. However, for the MBO process advocated here, my experience suggests that an active listening approach that incorporates problem solving and coaching be used. It is helpful to begin by asking the appraisee to comment on the past year and reflect on his or her ability to achieve the goals set previously. This should begin a dialogue on what happened, why, and what can be done to further goal achievement if indeed a problem exists. Although the interchange must be honest and should reflect actual behaviors and results, it is helpful to balance positive reinforcement with constructive criticism.

Beginning with the goal setting plans developed by the employee is appropriate because it should involve a comfortable area of discussion containing no real surprises, given the employee involvement in setting these goals. Years ago, Maier (1958) presented three methods of appraisal interviews: tell and sell; tell and listen; and problem-solving.

Tell and sell involves a manager-dominated interview in which an employee is talked to about what's good, what's not so good, and what to do about it. The manager does all the talking and the employee is supposedly convinced of the truth of the manager's point of view. *Tell and listen* involves distinct sets of communication, from the manager to the employee first, and then from the employee to the manager. This involves a form of two-way communication but no teamwork in deciding what issues need to be discussed or how to resolve concerns. *Problem-solving* appraisal interviews involve much more two-way communication so that both parties have an opportunity to define the agenda of the meeting and work toward mutually solving the issues that are identified. In this case, the employee is also active in creating a plan for defining improved performance.

To maximize the effectiveness of the appraisal interview, a blending of all three methods is appropriate; this is the practice in the MBO process. With MBO, information is communicated about performance, discussion is encouraged, a course of action is defined, and the employee is active in creating a plan of improved performance. The person conducting the interview should try to maintain eye contact, be responsive when the other person is speaking, ask many questions, and remember that stating concerns with a positive spin results in greater acceptance. For instance, instead of stating to a coach who is overly aggressive with officials, "You have a very bad temper with officials. Your behavior on the sidelines is ridiculous and I want it to stop!" the interviewer might say, "I am very interested in developing a supportive environment for officials and ensuring that our athletes show due respect. Let's talk about your role in providing leadership with respect to officials." The interviewer should be descriptive ("What do you think happened here?") as opposed to judgmental ("How could you have let such a stupid thing happen?"); and supportive ("What can we do to solve the problem, and how can I help?") instead of authoritarian ("This is what you're going to do to solve this problem."). The interviewer should also make specific and accurate comments, avoid exaggerations, and try not to interrupt when the other person is speaking. The following list summarizes the current thinking about communication styles that are fundamentally more acceptable to subordinates and that originated with the early research studies of W. Charles Redding (1972) and his graduate students at Purdue University (Cline & Wilmoth, 1987; O'Reilly & Anderson, 1980; Wheeless, Wheeless, & Howard, 1984). Better supervisors tend to be

- more open to and enjoy communicating with employees in meetings and when explaining instructions,
- better listeners, more approachable, and willing to listen to suggestions and complaints,
- less autocratic and more participative with instructions on getting things done,
- more sensitive to the feelings of others, and
- more open and willing to communicate information more often and in a timely fashion (Redding, 1972).

The interviewer's body language is also important. Body movement has an influential role in human communication, and supervisors should be aware of how their body language may be interpreted. The interviewer's interest and state of mind can be portrayed by nonverbal behaviors such as posture, eye contact, head position, and facial movements. Slouching, doodling with pen and paper, and staring at a spot on the wall often indicate boredom and lack of interest. A heavy sigh, raised eyebrow, and squinting of the eyes are likely to be interpreted as impatience, anger, disbelief, or even disgust. None of these modes of communication are likely to positively influence the evaluation meeting, especially when the manager is attempting an evaluation interview in which open communication is valued. Direct eye contact, attentiveness, and positive nonverbal and verbal feedback are important to fostering an environment conducive to two-way communication. Some categories of errors in body language include the following:

- **Eye contact.** Looking around often indicates inattentiveness and a lack of interest.
- **Body fidgeting.** Constant small body movements point to discomfort.

- **Making noises.** Heavy sighing or other noises under the breath suggest the potential for many negative feelings: disbelief, boredom, anger.
- **Drawing or doodling.** This indicates a "devil may care" attitude, boredom.
- **Making faces.** This is suggestive of many emotional states: anger, disbelief, mirth.
- **Body slump.** Slouching is unprofessional and condescending.

Earlier in this chapter I emphasized the importance of the goal setting meeting as a performance management opportunity to communicate positives, discuss problems, reinforce the department's mission, and provide motivation for the pursuit of future goals. This is achieved through proper preparation for the meeting and an understanding of the importance of effective modes of both verbal and nonverbal communication. It is very important that the positive aspects of an individual's performance be clearly stated, whether these involve the achievement of a set goal or other aspects of effective achievement. The manager should be prepared with a list of points that need to be imparted over the course of the appraisal interview, and care should be taken to start on a positive note. Discussions should start with positive statements such as, "I thought you did a really good job with such and such. I liked the way you handled x, y, and z, and feel this really positively helps us with this and that. How did you feel about. . . ? Again, I really appreciate your efforts in getting this done. Great job!" Of course, an evaluation is almost never 100 percent positive, and areas of concern also need to be addressed. If possible, problem areas should be discussed in a nonthreatening manner. Using the word *we* often softens the blow, in comparison to saying, "*You* have done something wrong or ineffectively." For example, "You know, Mark, I'm wondering about the way *we've* handled releasing players. I'm not so sure that cutting the team with lots of other players in the gym is the best way to handle that situation. I know this is a difficult problem with so many cuts to make, but do you think there might be a more private, considerate way to handle it?" Posing a problem that's stated as a problem that *we* have together and then defining a solution to the problem through mutual discussion is usually the most effective way to handle it. With a difficult problem or with people who are not willing to budge on their point of view, it helps to hear them out before discussing why it's very important for the organization to proceed in a different way. Using the example just noted, let's say Mark was really obstinate about changing how he goes about cutting his team. The supervisor needs to hear him out, and then provide direction, perhaps like this: "Mark, I know that the numbers provide a real problem for you. Let's look at it this way. As a department, we need to be as friendly and open to the athletes as possible. Our relationship with the student body as a whole is critical to our continued funding on campus. I know that some of the students feel that being taken aside in front of a group and told publicly that they've been cut is unfair. It's pretty traumatic from an ego point of view, and also is pretty impersonal. Perhaps you could use each of your assistants and set up three-minute appointments in the offices to meet privately with everyone being cut. Each coach could talk to one-quarter of the pool and provide each athlete some feedback about what to work on. Those being cut could leave the meeting with a positive message of 'Thanks for trying out,' and with hope that they will continue to work on their game, and would perhaps even come out and support the team. I think that this kind of approach is really important to the maintenance of a positive relationship with our students. I'd really like to give this approach a try."

This example ties the solution to a problem into the overall operating principles or mission of the department. Using the department mission is often an effective way to solve problems because it reinforces a collective way of operating based on the environment within which both the supervisor and the employee work. Being very specific, as in the examples provided here, where specific issues are presented and solutions are discussed, is also motivating. The easiest way to motivate an individual toward success is to arrive at concrete goals for achievement that are at once challenging but achievable, and that logically fit within the mission and objectives of the overall unit. In order to be motivated to change, people need to know why and how the change would benefit them and others. In my experience, motivation results from having clear objectives for achievement that are challenging but attainable, that matter to the overall organization, and that the individual has some say in developing.

At this point it is appropriate to comment on the assessment situation that goes awry, when the employee is angry or defensive. Spend time thinking in advance about how you will react to an unpleasant situation, and then what you might do to manage the employee's response. You need to maintain control of your own emotions because adding fuel to the fire is inevitably unproductive. Keeping your voice even and looking for ways to question and respond to the employee's point of view is necessary. If the employee interrupts with an angered or frustrated rebuttal to a point you are trying to make, go into active listening mode, ask questions, and hear the employee out before going back to your original line of thought. Do not ignore the unpleasantness or divert it to another time and place, because for an employee, there is usually nothing more frustrating than feeling the condescension of being brushed off. Begin by trying to restate the employee's point of view and acknowledging it. Then ask for more information about the employee's point of view. By allowing the employee the opportunity to vent, you will often defuse the situation. From there, clearly articulate the issue and attempt to find a way to move forward.

Closing comments to the assessment process should provide a summary of the core messages that have been communicated and should set the tone for future achievements. It is important that the major issues of the evaluation be discussed at closing. It is also important that the goals that will be the focus of the future review be restated. Wherever possible, the closing comments made by the supervisor should be positive and helpful, and they should clearly articulate expectations for the future. Try not to lay blame; try to stress the positive; describe specific problems briefly and objectively; try to reach a win-win position. Ensure that the employee has no further questions and tell the employee when the next meeting or evaluation step will occur. Walk the employee out in a friendly manner. The following is a sample script for closing the appraisal discussion.

Sample Script for Closing the Appraisal Interview

Karen, now that we've reviewed the entire appraisal, let me summarize our discussion and what I believe to be the key points. Is it fair to say that you believe (summarize the employee's response to the evaluation)?

As we have discussed I think your overall performance has been very strong. I am particularly impressed by (describe areas of strength). The one area that I would like to see you improve is (describe weakness that needs improvement).

We have both agreed that you will focus on the following three goals for next year (list the goals). We will have a midpoint meeting to see how you're progressing, and I will make the funding available for the computer technology course you need to pursue.

I think that's it for me ... do you have any further questions or concerns?

Thanks for your continued good work and all that you contribute to our organization. I look forward to meeting with you again in September.

Summary

This chapter presented information about performance appraisal procedures. It focused on how to develop a procedure, who should perform and provide input to the evaluation, and when and where it should occur. The chapter presented the reasons for using an MBO procedure for evaluating personnel in a sport organization, as well as information regarding the design, data collection, implementation, and optimization of the system. The chapter also addressed issues relative to the performance appraisal discussion and feedback meeting, and issues involved in gaining organizational support for the process.

Chapter 4 will discuss evaluating different categories of personnel in distinct classifications of sport organizations.

IN THE MANAGER'S SHOES

The Barrington Bears Hockey Franchise and Coach Bill Boyd

The Bears are the pride of small-town Barrington. The junior hockey team is singlemindedly supported by the 5000 or so citizens of the town. The team plays 52 conference games each year, followed by the playoffs.

As head coach, Bill has free reign to manage each component of the hockey club. He is responsible for all aspects of player personnel, team operations, and financial accountability. In fact, Bill Boyd is a one-man show for the Barrington Bears. He may not work the concession stand during the games, but he is responsible for its administration and all other details of event and facility management.

The owner of the team is Peter Mancini, a young entrepreneur and millionaire who made a fortune early in his career while working for a large computer manufacturing organization. Although Peter is pleased to allow coach Boyd free reign of the hockey franchise, he is interested in having a formal method of communicating with the coach. He also believes emphatically in the adage, "No goals, no glory."

After seeking the advice of an old friend in the human resources department of his former place of employment, Peter decides to build an MBO system of performance management as a tool to evaluate and communicate with his head coach. Describe the MBO system that Peter is envisioning by listing the steps involved in the evaluation procedure.

A Performance Appraisal Interview Turned Nightmare

Brian is the manager of the Get Fit Fitness Club and the direct supervisor of Michelle, a senior-level fitness instructor. Consider the following interview script of the evaluation meeting conducted by Brian with Michelle.

Brian: "Sorry I'm late. I'm swamped right now and don't have much time. Let me get right to the point. I don't think you're getting the job done just now. Your class attendance is down, you were late for work last Tuesday, and your choice of music is out of touch. I think you're losing your interest in this job and you know that young, energized employees are critical for success in the fitness industry. I want to know what you're going to do about it."

Michelle: "What I'm going to do about it? You can go fly, you idiot! I haven't the slightest idea what you're talking about. My class attendance is excellent, and is, in fact, the best in the organization. I was late for work last week because I was called in to a shift that wasn't mine because Karen became ill. You don't have a clue about what goes on around here."

Brian: "Now, Michelle, that's not true. Yesterday I heard two of our customers complaining that they don't like the music in your class. I don't think that you should pick the old stuff you like. What about the participants?"

Michelle: "Brian . . . this meeting is over. Why don't you check the records? You'll find the paper work on class votes for choosing music, and the evaluations by class participants on my demeanor in class, the content that's taught, and the perceived effectiveness of my teaching. Don't ever call me to a meeting like this again. And you're the one who shouldn't be late!"

Michelle gathers her things and walks out.

What mistakes has Brian made in this appraisal interview? Write a new script that will help Brian to open the meeting in a tactful and nonthreatening manner, but will also allow him to bring up these concerns: (a) Michelle's lateness, (b) the music Michelle uses in her classes, and (c) Michelle's commitment to the club and to teaching fitness in general.

The Hostile Appraisal Interview

It's 2:45 P.M. on a Thursday afternoon and Peter Wamsley is psyched up. He has just completed a third and final review of the performance appraisal agenda for Brett Gifford. He has a specific game plan for conducting the performance review meeting with Brett at 3:00 P.M. He knows that there has been a history of difficulty with this particular employee, and that he must be prepared for the denial and hostility Brett will surely express over the issue of Brett's communication style.

The fact is that Brett's colleagues and customers find him cold, uncaring, and condescending. Their perceptions have been clearly voiced, and Peter is convinced that the allegation is both true and universally held within the organization. Peter believes that Brett will deny the allegation and respond with anger, disgust, and his own allegation that "everyone is out to get me."

In preparation for the appraisal interview, Peter reviews his mental checklist of points that will help him manage a difficult and potentially hostile employee appraisal interview. What should be going through his mind?

See appendix C for reflections on the cases.

FOUR

Evaluating Sport Organization Personnel: Job Setting and Position Type

The importance of specificity has been a recurring theme in this book. As noted in previous chapters, every job must be analyzed before a meaningful job description can be developed, and valid performance appraisal criteria are those that emerge from the content deemed important for the particular position. In addition, an MBO goal-setting appraisal system is highly appropriate for assessing the performance of sport organization personnel because of the natural fit between this situation-specific methodology and the number, type, and setting of jobs within such organizations. The most common sport personnel positions (e.g., coaches, administrative managers, support staff) and the various settings (e.g., schools, clubs, national sport associations) in which they are found will be discussed in this chapter. Once again, the importance of specificity cannot be overemphasized. As discussed in earlier chapters, environmental factors internal to the organization can have a profound influence on an employee's ability to succeed at work. Factors of the external environment and the values attached to sport in society can also play a major part in evaluation. Let's take a closer look at sport in society and the values formed about sport that tend to influence the effective evaluation of personnel in sport organizations and their different settings.

Sport in Society and Personnel Evaluation in Context

Sport today is a universal phenomenon. It is inextricably linked to the major social institutions that regulate society, and most individuals are touched in some way by sport. The magnitude of the interest in sport and the undeniable link between sport and society (through government and politics, the economy and big business, the mass media, and the educational system) generate undeniable pressures for those working in sport. Such an environment can and frequently does contribute to personnel evaluations becoming one-dimensional in nature, played out in the media, and void of any actual performance data or foundation in fact. Because the consequences of evaluation can be monumental for the employee, administrators responsible for evaluation must be cognizant of and resistant to unfair appraisals.

Understanding the Environment

The first line of defense against a lapse into such an ineffective style of evaluation is an understanding of the environment that affects the organization or, in this case, the place of sport in society. As an example, let's compare Canada to the United States; although there are numerous similarities between sport administration in the two countries, there are also major differences. For instance, the role of the Canadian government in developing amateur sport is very different from the private enterprise system seen in the United States. In addition, the big business approach to American college sport is considerably different from the approach taken to sport in Canadian colleges and universities. Other differences in sport administration in different countries are apparent when we examine sport organizations in Europe, Australia, and Japan. It is important to understand the intricacies of the sport system and factors of the environment within which an organization works in order to effectively stage employee performance appraisal. Clearly, an in-depth look at the place of sport in societies around the globe is beyond the scope of this book. However, a look at some of the prevalent issues will help to clarify the importance of organizational setting as an issue that needs to be considered when evaluating sport personnel.

Influence of Cultural Settings

The cultural setting within which a sport organization exists will influence the organizational environment, and thus, this setting must be considered in the development of a performance appraisal system as well as in the delivery of human resource policy. In the United States, sport is undisputedly big business, and the professionalization of sport is incredibly pervasive. Over the years, sport sociologists have framed the concept of "pride in place" (Coakley, 1986; Goldstein, 1979; Nixon & Frey, 1996). They have contended that sport holds a prominent place in American society because people have a tendency to strongly affiliate with successful sport teams, and that people actually derive immense feelings of positive self-worth and accomplishment through a local sports team's exploits. The combination of big business financial stakes, mass media hype, and fervent fan attachment to teams tends to create a pressured, zero-sum evaluation philosophy defined by win-loss records and profit. Such a state of affairs is commonplace in American sport organizations and represents a significant challenge for effective and fair performance appraisal.

For many Canadians, sport is as much about participating as it is about watching, and is as focused on less visible amateur sports as it is on big business, professional sport (Hall, Slack, Smith, & Whitson, 1991). Sport in Canadian society is often seen as a meritocracy, as described by Birrell (1989): "Sport . . . based on skill quietly reaffirms our national common sense: Individuals who work hard and have the right stuff will always prevail. . . . Those who are at the top must have risen to the top through fair means, and thus deserve their position" (p. 213). The link between amateur sport and government and the delivery of sport through the education system and sport governing bodies quite possibly flavor the performance appraisal system designed in the Canadian context.

The European sport system is extraordinarily complex and continuously developing. The complexity of the system results from massive growth and great diversification since World War II (Camy, 1996). As in North America, sport is pervasive in Europe. It involves elite participation and fan spectatorship, as well as mass participation, leisure, fitness training, and education. High-performance sport is professional in nature, with a capacity for huge media exposure, organized from a business enterprise viewpoint. Competitive sport is community oriented, largely organized through a system of sport clubs and leagues. Educational sport also exists where sport is the principle component of physical education in the primary and secondary school system. The complexity of the system alone will emerge as a factor in human resource policy development because the different organizational missions and contextual factors of the environment must play a prominent role in helping to define the performance appraisal system.

Sport in Australia holds a particularly rich history and place of prominence in society, to the point of being a significant factor in promoting the national image. Sport has even, on occasion, been dubbed a "national obsession" by some, with millions of registered participants in more than 10,000 sport organizations. As such, the role of government in financing and organizing athletic competition has been prominent, as has the issue of passing financial responsibility from federal to state governments (Jobling & Deane, 1996). The system began as a community-based club structure, and the club structure continues to dominate today. However, a dearth of medals at several Olympic events during the 1970s prompted a national inquiry into the state of the sport delivery system and an expansion of government funding. At the same time, an interest in the professional management of sport delivery organizations emerged, resulting in a stronger emphasis on the professional preparation of sport management professionals in Australian universities (Shilbury, 1996). The Australian government responded to and promoted this renewed interest in elite-level performance by pouring more financial support into the development of national training centers, which in turn effected a reincarnation of the strategic management for sport through the training of professional sport management personnel.

Regarding sport in Japan, in recent decades, significant changes in the Japanese economy have translated into changes in the lifestyles of Japanese people and the growth of participation and interest in sport. Sport in Japan is delivered through a system of federal and municipal organizations such as the Japan Amateur Sport Association. In addition, professional sports clubs, an amateur sport club system, and private commercial sports facilities provide opportunities for willing participants. Sport leaders hold full-time positions within the sport system, and volunteers contribute to the organization of events and activities.

Two Key Issues for Performance Appraisal in Varying Contexts

Although differences exist in the delivery mechanisms for sport and the operational context of sport organizations in different countries, performance appraisal remains an important human resource function. The MBO system outlined in the previous chapters of this book can be useful in embracing the organizational setting. However, two important issues require comment in the discussion of sport in society and its relationship to performance appraisal in sport organizations. They are (a) the use of win-loss record as the sole criterion of success for measuring the job performance of sport personnel; and (b) the concept of linking personnel evaluation to the mission of the organization.

Measuring Success Through Win-Loss Records

The problem with the use of win-loss record as the ultimate criterion of success is that it produces two finite categories: one good, one bad. In reality, however, innumerable factors contribute to success. In other words, a loss may not be an indication of bad performance, and a win may not result from good performance. In the United States, and to a lesser degree Canada, evaluating personnel in sport organizations is confounded by the issue of success, because success in sport is defined through the ultimate criterion of winning and losing. Nonetheless, the win-loss record continues to be used consistently as the main basis for evaluation, and often as the number one factor in hiring and firing decisions, partially because win-loss is the easiest criterion to use: it's easy to obtain and, in raw form, is quantified. Because people in today's society identify to such a great extent with their professional teams of choice, they want, and "need," a winning team. If their need is not met, they seek a quick solution; the most popular quick solution is "Get rid of the coach!" The media, responsible for presenting public opinion and willing to heighten controversy, often adds force to the public pressure. In the absence of factual information about the coach's performance, a wave of public pressure roars into the offices of professional sport administrators, who often do not have any additional criteria with which to make coaching evaluations and decisions. With only the win-loss record as a criterion, they are apt to succumb to the wave of pressure by firing the coach.

Two major problems are at play in this scenario. The first problem is that a reliable coaching evaluation system may not be in place to guide the administration in this situation. The second problem is that the public is not aware of alternative coaching criteria on which to base their opinions. The solution to both of these problems, however, must begin with sport administration professionals. It is the responsibility of the sport professional who does personnel evaluation to broaden the base of evaluative criteria and then put them into practice in a systematic manner. Only when evaluation systems have been created and put to use consistently can the public and media be educated about coaching evaluation. Thus, it is incumbent on sport administrators to address the problems of inconsistent and arbitrary coaching appraisal. An organization without a solid evaluation system is a shaky one, susceptible to the unpredictable winds of public opinion.

Linking Mission to Performance Management

Along with the issue of winning and the impact this factor can have for the fair evaluation of sport personnel is the concept of linking the organization's mission to performance management. It is critical that evaluation policy and practice emanate from and align with the mission of the organization because the performance of personnel drives the effectiveness of the organization. This factor is often overlooked, but the inability to link personnel evaluation directly to the organization's mission has the potential to derail the entire system of performance appraisal. The assessment of factors unrelated or inconsequential to the mission of the organization, though without merit, continues to occur.

In defining their missions, sport organizations tend to emulate the mission and practices of the highest competitive level for a particular sport, which is often professional sport. However, the mission of a professional baseball franchise is likely very different from a Little League Baseball club; and it should be! It may be very appropriate to assess the performance of the Major League Baseball general manager on success factors such as tickets sold, profit margins, and overall organizational image. The same cannot be said for the individual organizing a sport club for children. Therefore, the evaluation criteria and procedures used for assessing the performance of various types of sport personnel should reflect the unique mission of the organization.

This trickle-down Big League effect is very common in sport. It is related to the major impact of the media's depiction of sport and individual athletes, and the impact that such notoriety has within our society. In effect, it produces stardom and hero status for accomplished professional athletes in the eyes of both children and adults. The sensationalization of former NBA basketball player Michael Jordan and the advertising campaign slogan of "I wanna be like Mike" is a case in point. The marketing of the persona of Michael Jordan and other professional athletes in many different sports brings a halo effect to professional athletes and their teams, and sport organizations and participants at virtually every level try to emulate the practices of the professional organization. However, if the missions of the two organizations differ, this may lead to ineffective management procedures, such as the ineffective evaluation of athletic personnel alluded to previously.

The following sections will focus on types of personnel to be evaluated in sport organizations.

Personnel to Be Appraised in Sport Organizations

Sport administrators, coaches, managers (such as marketing and sports information managers, and event coordinators), and support staff (such as athletic therapists, conditioning experts, sport psychologists, and equipment managers) must all be evaluated. It doesn't matter whether these individuals hold full-time paid or volunteer positions. Regardless of job status, performance appraisal is necessary to ensure appropriate supervision, to communicate feedback, and to maximize the accomplishment of the organization's mission. Let's investigate these positions in further detail.

Administrators

Administrators, the individuals responsible for managing the activities of the organization, play a momentous role in goal acquisition. The evaluation of their performance and subsequent communication of positive and negative feedback is critical for achieving organizational effectiveness. Their performance should be monitored and the results communicated.

Administrators in full-time positions should be assessed using the information and procedure presented in the earlier chapters of this book. That is to say, the roles and responsibilities emanating from a job assessment and defined within the incumbent's job description should articulate what is important within the job and what should be appraised. Then, an MBO procedure of goal setting and communication can be developed and implemented by the administrator's superior within the organizational structure. This superior might be an athletic director appraising the performance of a coordinator or manager; a personnel committee evaluating the performance of the executive director of a national sport organization; or a university vice president for student affairs assessing the accomplishments of a university athletic director. Several sources of input to the individual's performance should be acquired; the evaluation should be based on observations; behaviors should demonstrate the handling of specific situations, roles, and responsibilities as detailed in the administrator's job description. Sample job descriptions for athletic administrators are presented in appendix A.

Volunteer administrators should also be subject to evaluation. They are accountable for their actions and need regular communication concerning their performance. However, it is unrealistic to suggest that a sophisticated procedure be employed to assess how well an individual is "performing" his or her hobby. For this purpose it is recommended that a modified MBO procedure be used, engaging a personnel committee and implementing a single goals meeting per year. In the situation of a minor league hockey association president, a personnel committee might be composed of a parent, coach, and city administrator. Each member of the committee might seek information from his or her constituents regarding the progress of the organization and leadership of the administrator. If a job description does not exist, the goals meeting can serve to develop the criteria that success will be based on. A self-evaluation would also be useful. Even though the situation is volunteer and non-paid, the process is useful given the need for communication and the importance of individual accountability for making responsible decisions.

Although sometimes overlooked, administrators such as college athletic directors, presidents of sport clubs, or general managers of amateur or professional sport organizations need to be evaluated on job performance. The nature of the position, size and scope of the organization, and organizational mission should all be considered when formulating an evaluation system. The MBO procedure for evaluation, or a modification of it, will serve this group well. The volunteer president of the minor hockey association can be assessed by a committee of coaches, parents, and peer administrators. The criteria for appraisal will emanate directly from his position description and must include items for which he has control. The evaluation meeting would likely include an assessment of communication ability, planning and organizational skills, public relations, and fund-raising accomplishments, among others. The modified MBO procedure that involves a yearly meeting to accomplish goal setting and to foster communication is important for the volunteer administrator and for the sport organization.

Different from this, but of equal importance to the organization, is the assessment of administrators at a higher level of structure and competition, such as college athletics or professional sport. College athletic directors should be assessed on job description skills such as leadership, planning, organization, communication, rules compliance, and financial management. The success of the program, whether or not teams win championships, often receives heavy public debate and is seen by the layperson as an important assessment factor. However, valid evaluations must be anchored on the foundation of the organization. In addition, American college athletic programs are justifiably concerned with other indicators of success, such as student-athlete academic achievement, Title IX and compliance issues, or fund-raising accomplishments. Most importantly, the athletic director must be held accountable for items within the director's own control that are written and agreed to by way of the formal job description. The lack of success of the men's basketball team may or may not result from the performance of the athletic director. This caveat provides an important rationale for the development of job-specific performance criteria and the MBO system of performance management advocated in this book.

The same can be said for administrators of professional sport teams, with one exception. Appraisal for these individuals must begin not with the formal job description, but with the mission of the organization. For example, if the mandate of the organization is entertainment, and if the spectators' experience of "entertainment" is directly linked to a minimum attendance figure, and if the team's ability to win is also influenced by attendance and fan support, then the administrator's role in the competitive success of the team may be more of a factor. This type of administrator may, depending on the job description, be more involved in player personnel issues than a college athletic administrator. This might result in team success playing a heavier role in the overall evaluation of the administrator. This is appropriate given the mission of the organization. This does not mean that every sport organization administrator should be assessed as described in this example, nor does it mean that the win-loss record should constitute the only criterion of evaluation.

Head Coaches

The discussion on athletic administrators also applies to head coaches. Professional coaches employed full-time should be appraised based on their job description and as described in the earlier chapters of this book. However, one caution is reemphasized at this point: refrain from the natural tendency to put too much emphasis on performance outcomes as the best indicator of effective coaching performance. Winning and losing is merely one aspect of a myriad of factors contributing to successful coaching performance. A loss may result from unsuccessful coaching, but it may also result from circumstances outside of the coach's control, such as injuries, a close call by the referee, inclement weather, or just a bad bounce of the ball. These factors, though an inherent part of sport, are simply uncontrollable. Also worthy of consideration is the zero-sum nature of sport. For every winner there will be a loser. Neither winning nor losing is in itself a valid indicator of successful or unsuccessful performance by the head coach.

For every handful of professional coaches there are hundreds of volunteer coaches directing teams for all age groups. They also deserve to have their performance appraised given the importance that evaluation can play in the personal development of the coach and the accountability important to the constituents involved. The MBO goal setting approach detailed earlier, or a modification to streamline the process, will provide for the necessary two-way communication. A high school athletic director or principal may be responsible for the assessment of a volunteer scholastic coach. Several sources of input are still applicable. A national team coach might be appraised by a personnel committee after gathering athlete, assistant coach, and managerial feedback. The assessment in each case would be specific to the job description of the coach involved and to the goals set for achievement.

A recent study by Heather Barber and Jean Eckrich (1998) titled "Methods and Criteria Employed in the Evaluation of Intercollegiate Coaches" attempted to define criteria appropriate to evaluating college coaches in the United States. The categories of criteria defined by these authors for collegiate basketball coaches included the following: technical/skill development, fund raising, program success, public relations, coach/player relationships, administrative skills, role model, and support of student-athlete model. For American collegiate coaches, this work provides tremendous insight into defining appropriate criteria for evaluation purposes. A model for developing evaluation criteria for Canadian university coaches was presented in chapter 2. Sample job descriptions for several levels of head coaches are presented in appendix A.

Task-Specific Managers

Other positions typical of sport organizations warrant comment from the perspective of performance appraisal. Many college, university, provincial, state, national, and professional sport organizations employ marketing managers, sports information and communications personnel, and event management staff. These individuals might possess job descriptions similar to those illustrated in appendix A. The positions are integral to the overall operation and goal achievement of the organization and must also be appraised for performance. The MBO procedure described previously will benefit this group as well. The sources of input, however, should relate directly to the specific tasks of the job and the individuals the job incumbent comes in contact with. For instance, performance input specific to a marketing manager may be solicited from two or three of the major sponsor partners that the manager services. Members of the media may be asked to comment on specific areas of performance for the sports information person. These forms of input should be one facet of the data collected, not the only source. Observations, peer assessments, self-assessments, and content analysis of documents are also important sources of job-related performance. Again, self-evaluation is encouraged. One note of caution is appropriate to this category of assessment: job responsibilities among these positions are often blurred when successful performance is the result of extensive job overlap. The converse is true that unsuccessful performance may originate because of difficulties in another program area or as a result of factors of the environment. For example, the marketing manager may lose a supportive long-term sponsorship because a parent company may decide to redirect the corporation's advertising dollars, and thus the organization may inadvertently lose the advertising sponsorship of that company. This must not automatically be construed as mismanagement. An event management error attributed to the event personnel may originate from faulty communication between the marketing, sports information, and events managers. The point is that performance problems, especially as they relate to positions such as the ones listed above, must be sufficiently investigated to determine their specific causes before they can be improved. Most importantly, supervisors should perform the assessment based on the organization's mission and culture, the job assessment, job description, and goals set. MBO will benefit this group as a performance management tool, given the goal setting function inherent to the procedure and the task-oriented nature of these positions that lend themselves to MBO evaluations.

Support Staff

Sport organizations may engage both full- and part-time support staff. Assistant coaches, trainers, athletic therapists, equipment managers, and experts in mental and physical training are often integral components of both team and individual sport activities. These individuals may have part-time or full-time appointments or they may be honorarium or volunteer workers. In any case, some thought should be given to providing performance feedback to these people. For full-time support staff employees the MBO procedure will contribute the necessary goal setting and communication phase for effective appraisal. The hiring and assessment of assistant coaches is often felt to be the prerogative of the head coach. As such, the head coach should be involved in the assessment to a great degree, and the process should be completed in conjunction with the administrator responsible for evaluating the head coach. Team consultants or other part-time helpers such as sport psychologists and conditioning experts should be assessed by gathering feedback from the constituents involved. This feedback should be discussed with the support staff member each year. This is consistent with the modified MBO procedure described previously.

The bottom line is that a strategy for appraising and communicating performance to the employee, whether full-time, part-time, or volunteer, must be defined. The MBO procedure advocated in this book can apply in its entirety or it can be modified in an effort to streamline the process.

Of course, it's possible to use a different mechanism of evaluation such as the simple rating scale or checklist. You may be thinking, "MBO can't possibly be good enough to be used in every situation." In my experience,

MBO can be modified to include different rating scales or checklists as warranted by the situation, but it is still the best procedure for evaluating sport and recreation personnel, for three specific reasons: First, MBO is a system, a continuous process helping superiors and subordinates to communicate. This may not be the case with other methods. Second, MBO uses goal setting, making it an effective way to focus on what to achieve, along with providing a method to expedite communication that goes two ways within the organization. Third, MBO is situation-specific, and thus highly useful for sport organizations, which normally don't have large groups of employees completing the same tasks, as occurs in an assembly line operation in a factory. MBO is flexible, it's effective, and it's manageable when used as an ongoing performance management system.

Summary

This chapter discussed factors that often affect the development and implementation of effective performance appraisal systems specific to different organizational and cultural settings. In addition, it explored the consequence of both the role that sport plays in society and the importance placed on winning by society. The significance of situation-specific appraisal cannot be understated. This chapter described several different types of sport organization personnel for whom performance appraisal should be designed and the settings that dominate the delivery of sport in which these individuals work. It also presented information on evaluating specific managers in areas such as marketing, sports information, and event management, along with athletic administrators and coaches, both full and part time. Ideas specific to performance appraisal for team support staff like trainers, equipment managers, and sport psychology consultants were also offered.

Other issues also affect the development of performance appraisal systems. Managers need to be aware of legal and union issues, along with topics such as achieving employee support for the system and how to implement the system in their organization. These issues will be discussed in chapter 5.

IN THE MANAGER'S SHOES

Winning and the Performance of School Coaches

Members of the athletic advisory board of Clarington College Private School are in a quandary. The group is charged with defining the criteria on which athletic coaches will be evaluated, as no such criteria currently exist. In the past, coaches taught courses and organized and led their teams, and their evaluation was based mainly on their teaching effectiveness scores. But today, with increased interest in the high school's overall image and how that image can be enhanced through effective athletic department publicity, a move is being made to focus the workload of Clarington College coaches.

The athletic advisory board, consisting of nine wealthy alumni, is fixated on the issue of winning. Part of the group feels that there is no need for any other criteria. After all, if the team wins, could there be any other more important illustration of the effectiveness of the coach? Others on the committee feel that success can be measured in several different ways, and that winning contests is only one of several appropriate criteria for assessing the job performance of coaches.

As a human resources specialist brought in to guide the group, you have the job of clarifying this issue for the committee. How would you go about helping the committee to define effectiveness and specify the criteria for evaluation of the Clarington coaches? What issues would need to be discussed in order for the committee to set appropriate performance appraisal criteria in this context?

Evaluating Volunteer Staff

Karen lives in a small town with no official park district. As the mother of two elementary school children and someone who remembers her participation on community teams with pleasure, she is frustrated by the lack of organized sporting activities for her kids. Karen and two of her friends, who also have young children, decide to organize a youth soccer program and align with a neighboring town for competition. The idea is a resounding success, and within a few years the league has ten teams for four different age groups and a three-person executive committee responsible for organizing schedules, raising funds, and otherwise organizing the league. About 20 volunteers help out, some coaching the teams, others helping to car pool for games and practices, while others help organize and raise funds. All of the people involved volunteer their time.

Doug helps out by volunteering to coach. He's very good at it, and in fact coaches two different teams, a first- and second-grade team and a fifth- and sixth-grade team. Doug's youngest son also plays for the kindergarten-level team. Despite Doug's commitment to the kids and the league, problems are developing. Often, games on Saturday overlap, so he's still coaching one team while his second team is waiting to begin a game on another field. His son's games sometimes conflict with practice times, so more and more frequently he cancels practice so that he can watch his youngest son's games. It is apparent to Karen and her committee that Doug is spreading himself too thin. What can they do to solve this problem? Should there be an evaluation process for volunteer coaches, and if so, what should the process consist of? Karen is worried that Doug will be sensitive to criticism that he is taking on too much and wants to avoid losing Doug as a coach. She knows that a lack of volunteer coaches could lead to the soccer league folding. What can she do to alleviate this problem without alienating her volunteers?

See appendix C for reflections on the cases.

FIVE

Performance Appraisal in Sport Management: Other Issues

The groundwork has been laid; the two most critical components contributing to the development of an effective performance appraisal system have been presented. First, developing a knowledge bank of evaluation practices, procedures, and critical elements will enable the manager to design and implement an excellent performance management system. Second, incorporating information that is critical to the sport environment, and that sport managers must consider specifically for their organizational setting, will contribute immensely to the effectiveness of the evaluation system. However, as is often the case, managers must be aware of several other issues when developing and implementing performance appraisal. The following sections discuss some of the issues that have the greatest potential to influence the success of the performance appraisal system.

"Buy-In"

Achieving consensus that the newly created or adapted performance appraisal system is a positive move for the organization is very important if the system is to be effective. Because evaluation is meant for all employees and is a sensitive issue to begin with, it is important to be aware of the views of the constituents from the beginning. Gaining consensus means that a majority of those involved, whether rater, ratee, or management personnel, will believe that performance is managed better than it used to be. This will mean different things to different people. Senior managers will be concerned with furthering organizational goals. Line managers will want a system that enables them to better communicate information in a less threatening environment: a system for which the time invested is justified and worthwhile. Those who are evaluated will need to see the benefits of knowing exactly where they stand, how to improve their performance, and how to get ahead. At the same time, human resource managers and legal staff will be concerned that appraisals are both accurate and legal.

The first step to achieving buy-in is gaining recognition and acceptance of the need for the development of an evaluation system where one did not previously exist. Those affected by the performance appraisal system must agree with the need to upgrade a system considered unsatisfactory. Widespread understanding of the benefits of performance appraisal from the point of view of the stakeholder will initiate the buy-in process. With a positive organizational attitude about the whole concept of performance appraisal achieved, consultation and inclusiveness become important considerations. It is recommended that, along with the collection of their input and feedback, employees be involved in system design and implementation from the beginning. Clear articulation of the ultimate goals of the system, a time line for its development, and a task-oriented approach will facilitate the process. Compromise may be necessary. However, buy-in is worth the consideration. There is no point in having a system that is mistrusted, patronized, or ignored. It is critical that both the organization and its employees understand the system, perceive it as fair, and believe that, with cooperation, positive outcomes will accrue. According to McKirchy (1998) this should be viewed as creating "same-side-of-the-desk thinking." Consider the vignette on page 99 about the Jackson City Department of Recreation.

Unions

In some organizations employees belong to a union that represents and bargains for their collective rights. To enhance the potential for buy-in and same-side-of-the-desk thinking as presented earlier, labor union personnel need to be included in the design and communication process. Unions often represent a significant number of employees and negotiate collective agreements between the work force and administration. To develop an

An Example of How to Achieve "Buy-In"

Susan Smith is the director of parks and recreation for Jackson City. Susan has been unhappy with the tools used to evaluate her staff for each of the four years she has held the position of director. Performing personnel evaluations yearly has been most distasteful. Everyone gets defensive, nothing good for the employees or her department seems to come of the process, and overall distrust, fear, and even paranoia seem to invade the unit around performance appraisal time. With the support of the senior management of Jackson City, Susan decides to dismantle the current evaluation procedure; however, policy dictates that she must evaluate her staff on an annual basis and she understands the inherent value in doing so given her strong background in human resource management. Susan also knows that the major hurdle she must overcome is the attitude of her staff toward being evaluated. How does she get them to believe performance appraisal will benefit them as well as the organization?

Susan decides to invest some time in defining a strategy for change. Her unit consists of 28 employees and exists within a unionized environment that is halfway through a three-year collective agreement. She feels comfortable proceeding without a consultant and has strong support from senior management. With the resolve to achieve acceptance for evaluation within her organization, she defines the following strategy:

Step 1: Begin a process of informal consultation with the formal and informal leadership of the collective organization.

There are five department heads (the management team) that Susan meets with formally on a weekly schedule and individually twice a month; she also has occasion to discuss issues with them informally now and then. Susan decides to gather their input as to whether change is necessary. She is almost certain that she will be supported but wants to gather ideas informally about what changes should take place. She needs to be sure of the attitudes regarding performance appraisal held by her managers. At the same time, Susan chooses a staff member from within each department whom she knows to be a respected leader among peers, and she sets a schedule to gather their thoughts about other meetings and events. Susan considers this step "informal consultation," and knows it is critical to achieving employee support.

(continued)

(continued)

Step 2: Formally communicate the need for, and interest in, change.

Susan announces her change plan first to her management team and discusses the issue of "buy-in." The team then decides to draft a list of concerns employees have about the current system, and then a second list that defines the goals of evaluation: what could be achieved for both the employee and the organization through evaluation? This information is then taken to department meetings by the respective department heads; hard-copy handouts are distributed, and then a meeting of the whole organization is called within two weeks.

The goal of this series of meetings is communication: to float ideas and to gather feedback, to ensure that everyone is involved from the beginning, to educate everyone in the organization about the overall goals of the process, and to collectively move the process forward.

Step 3: Form a performance appraisal task force.

The committee will be chaired by a human resource specialist, and it will have membership as follows: five department heads; five elected members, one from each department; Susan as director of parks and recreation; and one member from the employee union. The membership of the committee is an important factor in achieving support throughout the organization. Committee size is manageable, and members of each department are represented by an elected colleague. The union is also represented from the beginning. The first piece of business for the members of the task force will be education. The task force will draw up a meeting schedule for the next two months, with an average of two meetings per week.

Step 4: Ensure regular feedback on the progress of the task force.

In an attempt to ensure buy-in from the managers and employees, the elected member of the committee will inform department members each week about the progress of the task force.

Step 5: Test the system.

The new evaluation method will be tested with one department in order to reduce the anxiety about the system before it is used throughout the organization.

Although much remains to be done, the plan for communication, consultation, and education will help Susan achieve the necessary support for change.

acceptable performance appraisal system, the system must be compatible with the needs, values, and expectations of its users. Thus, the union representatives, whose responsibility it is to voice and negotiate on behalf of their constituents, must be consulted throughout the process. If compatibility between the system and its users is to be achieved, union involvement is necessary.

Legal Considerations in Performance Appraisal and Enhancement

Successful human resource management can only be built on solid human relationships that are both mutually satisfying and beneficial. However, personal relationships between those who manage and those whom they manage do not stand alone as the only influences on how performance appraisal is conducted. There is always a legal environment that governs, to varying degrees depending on the jurisdiction, how individuals may act when attempting to evaluate and improve job performance. Although it is not feasible to outline here a complete list of legal considerations, there are a number of commonalities that apply. Two important kinds of legal factors should always be borne in mind when engaged in performance appraisal.

Legislative Influences

Employment exists within the legislative boundaries of the jurisdiction that an organization and its employees and managers live and work within. Every sport organization is subject to the legislative measures that govern the way that citizens must be treated. For example, your national, regional, and perhaps even local governments may all have human rights codes or constitutions that describe what is considered fair treatment of people. The impact of these overarching laws does not stop at the entrance to the gym or the office building you and your staff work in. They are the foundation that the details of working relationships are built on. They are easy to understand and to implement, for they make a simple case. When appraising someone's job performance, that appraisal must be grounded in criteria that are job-related. Everyone has the right to equal treatment without discrimination because of race, ancestry, color of skin, or marital status (just to name a few of many).

Statutory language does vary from place to place, and every sport manager should be well-versed in local legal requirements. Virtually all statutes can be found on-line via the World Wide Web, and the local library and city hall are other potential sources of legal information. In general, statutory language applies to all phases of the employment process. The effects of legislation affect the ways that an organization searches for employees; the ways that prospective employees are interviewed or tested; the ways that staff are trained once on the job and provided development and advancement opportunities; and the means by which workers are laid off, suspended, or dismissed. Typically, legislation is not written for the purpose of punishing organizations. Rather, it is designed to lessen or remove unfair practices and provide a remedy to individuals who have been the victims of inequitable practices. Most commonly, legislation is the backbone of protection against discrimination and retaliation. A performance appraisal process that neither discriminates nor retaliates against its employees is unlikely to run afoul of any legislative constraints on its practices.

Contractual Influences

Employment also exists within contractual boundaries. Even when no formal document has been written, there are inevitably some terms of employment that members of staff are expected to abide by and that the organization they work for is expected to conform to. The contract may be one negotiated by a single person or it may be one that applies collectively to a group of individuals who together have bargained with the organization.

A contract is an agreement between two or more people that creates obligations. These may be obligations to do certain things or not to do certain things, and it is vital that a sport manager know about the contractual strictures that guide an employee's understanding of what kind of performance is expected and how it will be assessed. Any contract will have what are called its *express terms*, specifically stated articles that define expected behaviors. These may appear in the contract itself, but may also appear in documents that the contract refers to, such as handbooks or policy documents that describe workplace rules. A contract will also have what are called its *implied terms*, categories of behavior that are assumed to be understood as expectations even when they are not expressly stated. For example, unless a contract specifically states otherwise, it is reasonable for a manager to expect an employee to obey lawful rules and carry out lawful orders of the employer. It is also reasonable for an organization to expect its staff not to engage in behavior that has a negative impact on the organization's interests (e.g., drunkenness on the job or harassment of another employee).

Differences exist in the ways that individual contracts and collective agreement contracts affect performance appraisal. In the case of individual contracts that do not specify to the contrary, an employee can be dismissed without further employer obligation if there is just cause to do so. One aspect of just cause is unsatisfactory performance such as habitual neglect of duty, incompetence, or disobedience of lawful orders. However, an individual contract may also be terminated without just cause as long as the employee is provided with reasonable notice of the termination. The latter form of termination is different in a collective agreement environment in which the legal relationship is not between manager and employee but between the organization and the collective bargaining unit. In such circumstances, dismissal for cause remains possible, but termination with reasonable notice is usually not, and collective agreements are inevitably very clear on what constitutes just cause and how it will be determined whether just cause exists.

Navigating Legislation and Contracts in Performance Appraisal

Although the legal environment can be complex, a few basic principles can help to guide sport managers through an appraisal process that avoids legal pitfalls:

- Set objective standards for performance and communicate these clearly and accurately to those being appraised.
- Provide regular and honest assessments of the work done by each employee so that there is no doubt in anyone's mind as to what has been said in the appraisal.
- When performance fails to achieve the desired standards, provide a well-defined pathway, including timelines, by which performance will be helped and expected to improve.
- Where performance is unacceptable or unsatisfactory to a sufficiently important degree, written reprimands that specify the problem and how it must be addressed are essential.
- Where disputes arise, ensure that the basic principles of natural justice are followed. In particular, someone who is being appraised negatively has the right to know the full details of the case against him or her and has the right to respond to that case. Also, anyone has a right to an unbiased decision maker when disputes arise. This is especially important in small organizations where everyone knows everyone else and it is sometimes difficult for objectivity to be maintained. Even then, however, it is reasonable for an employee to expect that a decision made about his or her performance is being made without any reasonable apprehension of bias.
- Finally, formulate an appeal process to provide a means by which an employee may challenge the content or process of an appraisal

perceived to be unfair. Depending on the size and circumstances of your organization, the appeal process might simply involve allowing the individual to append written comments stating his or her side of the story. In addition to this process, develop a formal grievance procedure. This involves an alternative dispute resolution procedure such as the peer review grievance panel, systems of complaint mediation, binding arbitration, or creating a position of organization ombudsman. Such a process can help to mediate issues before they become full legal disputes. Normally, disputes that challenge the mechanics or procedures of the performance appraisal system can be handled effectively using the internal grievance method. However, complaints about the fairness of a specific rating are not handled by peer review, and the burden of proof for providing the evidence to overturn a rating lies with the employee. In the absence of compelling evidence to suggest otherwise, the organization must support the leadership provided by its manager and his or her appraisal, or badly undermine that leadership. Of course, the ultimate appeal process for the employee is the legal system. It is hoped, however, that with proper training and a specific system for appraisal, many disputes about performance ratings can be effectively handled within the organization through an appeal process. For further information on the development of an appeal process to the performance appraisal system see Grote (1996). It might also be advisable to secure legal counsel to provide advice specific to your organization and to ensure that an appropriate appeal system is defined.

Overview of Labor Law in North America

It's clear that conducting performance appraisal ultimately involves making decisions about people; therefore, managers must have a good understanding of how the law affects human resource management. Labor and employment laws will apply from each of the provincial, state, and federal jurisdictions. Laws specific to the jurisdiction and country involved must be researched and applied. Because provincial and state laws vary, the following examples will focus on federal laws that apply to conducting performance appraisal in both Canada and the United States. These sections are intended to provide a brief overview. Sport managers are encouraged to be aware of applicable laws and to seek professional legal advice to ensure the legality of any performance management system and the appropriate treatment of all employees.

Canada

Canadian employment law is often referred to as a "legal jungle" because it consists of a network of labor-related regulations and laws set in 14 different jurisdictions: 10 provinces, 3 territories, and the federal government. As they apply to conducting performance appraisal, these laws prohibit discrimination based on race, religion, ethnic or national origin, sex, and marital status (Stone & Meltz, 1988). The Canadian Human Rights Act and Employment Equity Act preside from the federal government jurisdiction, with the provinces and territories directing employment and labor standards. Both types of laws are subject to constant change as new regulations are enacted and as the courts interpret existing laws.

According to Dolan and Schuler (1987) the following items will contribute to a legally defensible performance appraisal system in Canada:

- Evaluation decisions must not differ on the basis of race, gender, color, national origin, marital status, sexual orientation, creed, or age.
- The appraisal must be conducted within a formalized, standardized system.
- Appraisal criteria should emanate from job analysis.
- Data that appraisal decisions are based on must be objective and uncontaminated whenever possible, and rating on traits should be avoided.
- Several sets of observations on several criteria dimensions should feed the appraisal process.
- Raters must be trained on all aspects of performance appraisal.
- More than one evaluator should provide appraisal input.
- Specific performance standards should be communicated to employees.
- Employees should be afforded every opportunity to review their appraisals.
- An appeal system should be provided to enable a review of the appraisal in the event of disagreement.

The United States

Since the passage of the 1964 Civil Rights Act, performance appraisal has been viewed as an employment test and scrutinized in a manner similar to hiring, promoting, compensating, or terminating employees (Grote, 1996; McKirchy, 1998; Swan, 1991). The legal requirement for performance appraisal includes the need for the appraisal to emanate from job analysis, to be both valid and reliable as a measure of actual performance, and to be an ongoing and equitable process. The performance appraisal system must have no adverse impact on areas covered by law, such as an employee's race, sex, sexual orientation, religion, origin, age, or handicap status. Measurement standards are important and considered valid when it can be proved that (a) the person must be able to perform the task to do the job; and (b) the relationship between rating scores and skills needed on the job and the measurement of job performance exists.

The four major government agencies involved in American civil rights enforcement are the Equal Employment Opportunity Commission (EEOC), the Civil Service Commission, the Department of Labor, and the Department of Justice. According to Grote (1996) the major laws affecting the process of performance appraisal include the following: Civil Rights Act of 1964; Executive Order 11246; Age Discrimination in Employment Act; Rehabilitation Act of 1973; Uniformed Services Employment and Reemployment Act of 1994; Americans With Disabilities Act; Civil Rights Act of 1991; and Civil Service Reform Act of 1978. In summary, these laws require that performance appraisal systems incorporate the following points:

- Any measurement used to differentiate between employees must be valid and fairly administered.
- Certain skills must be shown to be valid, true, and necessary components of the job; in other words, performance appraisal criteria must be derived through job analysis and must be contained within the job description.
- Performance dimensions should be described in behavioral terms, and the rater must be able to consistently observe the employee performing assigned tasks.
- Raters must be trained to assess performance accurately.
- The system should provide for an appeal process in the event of a perceived unfair appraisal.
- The employee's right to privacy must be considered.
- Records must be accurate, relevant, and current.

Fortunately, the processes that create an effective performance appraisal environment are the same processes that protect sport managers from legal repercussions. Following a fair and thorough process untainted by personal bias is not simply a means to an end—that end being a sound appraisal of job performance. Fairness should be an end in itself: behaving in a way that is ethically in harmony with the laws that guide us on how to behave toward one another. Sound legal practice becomes sound performance appraisal practice.

Considering the final point of the list—that records must be accurate, relevant, and current—let's take a closer look at the issue of documenting the evaluation.

Documentation

The importance of collecting and recording data to accurately assess a person's performance must not be understated and is critical to the entire performance appraisal system, beyond mere legality. Observations, data collection, and the documentation of the information collected will provide the basis on which the performance appraisal is written. It begins with the written job description that was derived from the job analysis. The job description must be current and accurate. Next, information must be accumulated on the criteria agreed on for assessment through document content analysis, objective outcome data, behavioral observations, and other critical incidents of the job (Grote, 1996). Data from other evaluative sources also need to be collected and summarized with the contents of the supervisor's evaluation and the self-evaluation. This information will form the appraisal file and lend credence to the written performance document.

Rating Problems

Errors in rating the performance of an employee must be guarded against. Of primary importance to safeguarding the results of the appraisal process is an understanding of the types of rating errors that commonly occur. Some categories of common rating problems include the following:

- **Attribution bias.** Tendency to attribute failure to the individual and success to the situation.
- **Central tendency.** Propensity to rate individuals as average when performance is clearly higher or lower than an average rating.
- **Contrast effect.** Inclination to evaluate individuals in comparison to one another instead of in comparison to the standards of the job.

- **First impression error.** Tendency of the manager to make a first impression of an employee that will thereafter distort the impression of actual performance.
- **Halo or horns effect.** Inappropriate generalization, positive or negative, from one aspect of performance that then flavors all other areas of performance.
- **Negative and positive skew.** Rating all individuals higher or lower than is warranted; the opposite of central tendency.
- **Recency effect.** Practice whereby minor but most recent events have a larger impact than more major events that happened months ago.
- **Similar-to-me effect.** Tendency of raters to rate individuals similar to themselves higher than others.
- **Stereotyping.** Propensity to ignore individual differences and generalize findings across all groups of employees.

Adapted from Grote (1996).

Managers conducting effective performance appraisals will compile comprehensive and accurate information over the entire evaluation period, on agreed-upon criteria, from several sources of feedback. These managers must also have the courage and support of upper management to deliver negative appraisals when they have been earned. Whether motivated by cowardice or kindheartedness, inflated appraisals are detrimental to everyone involved and ultimately ruin the credibility of the performance appraisal system.

Along with the rating problems discussed above, there are errors of implementation that can be made regardless of the method being used. According to Swan (1991) the most common appraisal errors include: inadequately defined performance standards and criteria; an overemphasis on recent performance; the rater relying on gut feelings; insufficient or unclear performance documentation; misunderstandings surrounding the performance standards and criteria; inadequate time for discussion and too much talking by the manager; and lack of a follow-up plan. In addition to these potential pitfalls, an appraisal system that is not organized enough to ensure that the necessary steps occur in a timely sequence during the review period is destined to fail.

Training

The best performance appraisal system in the world will fail if those responsible for implementing it are not sufficiently trained to use the procedure. It is important that the managers with the responsibility for appraisal be trained, and it is also necessary that all others within the organization receive some orientation to the process. Training is necessary for two basic reasons: First, and quite obviously, to provide the knowledge and skills to use the performance appraisal system well. Sport managers should not assume that such training has been completed during basic managerial training. The second reason training is necessary is to ensure that the organization's human resource management processes are legally defensible. Within the organization, it's important that the entire management team, including senior managers, understand the performance appraisal system. Effective performance appraisal will cascade through the entire organization and thus become a universal function for all managers. In very small organizations, this may involve only one or two individuals. In larger organizations, the involvement of senior managers will lend support for the importance of investing in appraisal and address, from the top down, why it's important to give clear directions and feedback, and why goal setting and employee performance and achievement are such critical components of organizational effectiveness.

In the best case scenario, the training should be completed by those who helped to develop the appraisal process, or the implementation team. These are the people most suited to answering the questions that normally arise about the process because they were involved in developing and implementing it. In smaller organizations, the training might be completed by the individual responsible for human resources, or the head of the organization. If no one within the organization is qualified or comfortable with conducting training, a hired consultant can lead the organization through the implementation and training sessions.

Of course, the agenda for training is critical. To do performance appraisal well, and specifically to embark on MBO evaluation, requires that those evaluating have technical, people, and planning skills. Technical skills include an understanding of the entire performance management system and the ability to appraise performance objectively and accurately; the ability to recognize various levels of performance and to differentiate between good and bad; the competence to help others set goals and identify priorities; the capacity to help others define critical pathways and time lines for goal achievement; and the aptitude to coach subordinates in need of feedback and support.

Effective training for performance appraisal also covers the people skills that will be required, such as negotiating, coaching, and motivating. It is especially important that managers learn how to listen well, deliver threatening information with care, and communicate with clear, concise, and specific language. Training needs to cover the easy and mundane (e.g., filling out the forms) along with the exceptionally difficult (e.g., mustering the courage to discuss substandard performance in a candid, straightforward way). Finally, training for MBO needs to impart an understanding of the overall, multi-year process, as well as methods for defining a critical path and time line to facilitate the entire process. Training the appraisers to effectively understand how to develop good time lines goes hand in glove with understanding the philosophy behind conducting MBO and the overall goal of the organization.

One of the most effective modes for conducting actual training sessions involves role playing. Some people will be uncomfortable with taking part, but role playing is very effective in permitting learners to practice an appraisal interview, a chance to rehearse tough conversations and to learn what to say and what not to say. Role playing is most effective when two individuals work with a coach for guidance and when they work together for short periods of time. Depending on the situation, observers may or may not be involved. Another method of training involves behavior modeling, in which learners watch something being done in a preferred way, rehearse the situation, and then imitate the model. If live modeling is not possible, scripts of effective behaviors and dialogue can be used in training.

It Works

Remember that it *is* possible to develop and implement an effective appraisal system for the sport organization, even if the organization is one in which no evaluation system, or a dysfunctional one, currently exists (see "Key Information for Making the Performance Appraisal System Work," page 112). Beyond feasibility, however, a larger issue is at hand: necessity. The field of sport management has made remarkable progress over the last 50 years, adapting administrative practices from the field of business management and tailoring them effectively and admirably to the athletics realm. However, evaluation has been largely ignored. Several reasons have been cited to explain why personnel evaluation is particularly difficult in the sports setting. Although the obstacles to systematic assessment are real and many, the time has come to stop talking about them and to begin overcoming them.

Systematic evaluation is no longer merely an option; it is an essential component in the ongoing growth and development of sport organizations and their employees around the world. Why is it essential? Because the benefits that accrue are key components of a healthy organizational environment in which loyal, achievement-oriented employees are actively working to fulfill their part in the organization's mission. The successful organization that achieves its mandate does so with employees who have a stronger sense of belonging, employees who believe in their role in the organization's overall success. Such employees often thrive in an environment in which two-way communication is the norm and in which information sharing is an expectation.

It may seem counterintuitive at first to suppose that a personnel evaluation system might facilitate an open, communicative organizational culture. Based on past experience, one might expect the opposite. However, let's not forget that in the past, for the most part, personnel evaluation was not conducted effectively or consistently. Without an effective system, positive results could not possibly accrue. But now, we have a system that will yield countless benefits. The MBO system, if implemented systematically, can ultimately nurture a teamwork-oriented atmosphere. With increased awareness that goal setting is part of the yearly work cycle and that all employees are taking part in this system, the fear of discussing goals gradually decreases. The issue of goals and objectives, previously considered highly threatening to the individual and often avoided in conversation, becomes much less threatening when discussed within the evaluation framework. The focus has been transferred from the individual to the process of continual improvement and movement toward goals. The fearful mentality of the past is replaced with a team mentality that says, "We're all a part of this mission, working toward our respective goals and those of the organization as a whole."

In addition, the evaluation system provides people with a common language to discuss goals and objectives. Once everyone has begun to employ goal setting as part of the yearly work cycle, a stronger and more realistic understanding develops among employees. "The team" becomes aware that in any given year, each "player" will achieve some goals and fail to achieve others. Facing that reality and having a nonthreatening means of communicating about it provides the organization with something it never had before. In this way, subtly, the culture of the organization begins to change. A more open, teamwork-oriented atmosphere predominates.

The development of such an effective culture of organizational communication can result from the performance appraisal system that has been the focus of this book. An organization that maintains a work force in which effective communication is one cornerstone, and teamwork another, is an organization built like one of the Great Pyramids: destined to survive many changes in the environment over many years.

Key Information for Making the Performance Appraisal System Work

1. Ensure that performance appraisal is a year-round process that integrates a series of important activities and processes for the organization.

2. Each year, reflect on the criteria for evaluation, ensuring that they are representative of the current job. Also ensure that a balance of criteria reflective of behaviors, the outcomes of behaviors, and maintenance of the work environment are included.

3. Actively listen to the concerns of those involved with the process, including both managers and employees. Be aware that their concerns may be justified, and changes to the procedure can quickly result in their increased support for performance appraisal.

4. Make sure that everyone in the organization is educated about the process. Also make sure that managers are appropriately trained to direct and oversee the evaluation process.

5. Ensure that the performance appraisal system is action-oriented. That is, it is important that employees see that evaluations produce action within the organization. Promotions and pay raises are common action outcomes; however, internal accomplishment awards, enhanced support for training or professional development, and job changes are also effective consequences of performance appraisal that give the process credibility and motivate employees to achieve.

6. Finally, regularly evaluate the system itself. Ensure that the system is updated, altered, and manipulated based on the times and climate within which the organization is operating. Reviewing the evaluation system is an important step toward making performance appraisal work in the long run; this step is often overlooked.

Summary

This chapter discussed several issues that can affect the implementation of a performance appraisal system. In order for a system to be implemented, those who are to be evaluated must support it. Effectively working with unions and having knowledge of points of law will ensure that the evaluation system is fair, equitable, and legally defensible. Ensuring optimal methods for documenting the appraisal, having an understanding of rater problems, and training are also important safeguards. The chapter concludes with a discussion of the positive effects that performance appraisal can have on organizational and employee development: that is, making it all work.

◀ IN THE MANAGER'S SHOES

A Further Look at Hawkley Golf & Country Club

The first person to hold the position of marketing manager at Hawkley Golf & Country Club was Arnold Mazer. He held the job for 16 years and was a hard worker with enviable marketing skills. He was well known and well liked. Arnold built a superb marketing system from the ground up. As a result of "Arnie's" efforts and marketing talent, Hawkley grew in membership and profitability to become the most sought-after country club in the area.

The board of directors would have liked to have had Arnie on board for life. They assumed he felt the same way, but their assumptions were wrong. Arnold unexpectedly took a job with another club that offered him a similar position with a $10,000-per-year raise. He told the board of directors that, though he had enjoyed his years at Hawkley immensely, he needed a change.

However, in private, Arnie told a different story to his friends. He said it was not the money or the need for change that had prompted him to leave. For years, he'd felt unappreciated at Hawkley. He confided,

> "Don't get me wrong. I always felt appreciated by the members and sponsors at the club. But the board did not appreciate the work I did day-in and day-out for 16 years. They only spoke to me once a year, when we had the annual meeting. They shook my hand, gave me a Hawkley token of appreciation, and said, 'Keep up the good work.' It was a formality. I have drawers full of 'tokens' of Hawkley appreciation but not once did I ever actually feel appreciated by those people. There was never any feedback on all the marketing initiatives I poured my blood and sweat into. They didn't have enough time to ask how it was done. Likely, they were too busy determining their monthly profits. The bottom line—that seemed to be all they were looking for. Oh—that and the 'Hawkley image.' They referred to that 'Hawkley image' so many times, but not one of the staff that I spoke with had any idea what it

(continued)

(continued)

meant. If I had to take a guess at the image portrayed by the board of directors, I'd say the Hawkley image involves walking around occasionally with an air of aloof superiority."

In the end, Arnie left honorably and quietly, as was his way.

Consider the positive ramifications that would result for Hawkley and Arnie through the establishment of an MBO-style evaluation system. Define the problems that ultimately led to Arnie seeking a job change, but that might have been solved through better communication and reinforcement.

Cynthia Carrington and Hawkley Golf & Country Club

Arnie's replacement was Cynthia, who had all the credentials and experience deemed desirable for the position. As her first task, she began an extensive marketing research project in an effort to work toward long-term improvement in the marketing area. She decided to maintain the status quo in all other aspects of her job for the first year, trusting that short-term compromise was necessary for long-term progress. Accordingly, she performed the other facets of her job adequately.

Cynthia worked independently in her efforts, as Arnie had, for there was no one to report to. Her guides were the job description and the job performance forms that had defined the expectations placed on Arnie (see "Director of Marketing—Hawkley Golf & Country Club," pages 51-52). Because time lines were not mentioned in either of these documents, Cynthia drew her own time lines. Past experience told her these were reasonable and necessary for long-term success in such a setting. She proceeded with confidence. During her first year, club memberships and sponsorships declined slightly, almost immeasurably.

Unbeknownst to Cynthia, the board of directors was concerned that Cynthia was not doing her job. The bottom line did not look promising. Figures showed a slight decrease in revenues and a substantial increase in marketing expenditures. They had no idea where all the money was going. In the annual meeting, Cynthia received no Hawkley tokens of appreciation but she did receive a lot of questions. When asked about finances, Cynthia described her marketing research project, which was costly. She guaranteed the board that she would soon have results from the research project. When asked what she had done to enhance Hawkley's image, Cynthia responded, "Nothing. I can't improve an image that I have no information about. After analyzing the marketing research results, I assure you I will then have the groundwork on which to build a solid, lasting image for Hawkley." The board members were shocked at this. Next, one board member displayed the promotional materials that Cynthia had produced, asking why they looked so much like last year's. Cynthia provided her rationale regarding short-term compromise in some areas to ensure long-term progress in all areas. The board of directors did not look impressed.

The following week, Cynthia was called into another meeting with two board members. They informed her that they needed someone who would work on the image of the club, improve membership, and show bottom-line results. They told her she was not quite the type of person they needed at this time. She would have one more month to clear things up, and during that time, the board would find another marketing manager who was more "in line with the image and philosophy of Hawkley."

Feeling she'd been unjustly treated, and wondering what the heck "Hawkley philosophy and image" were anyway, she filed a lawsuit against the club. Her lawyer was confident Cynthia had solid grounds for what was termed "unlawful dismissal."

List the mistakes that the Hawkley board made in their dealings with Cynthia. Define the role that the following three factors play in preventing legal challenges to human resource decisions: (a) organizational structure, (b) communication, and (c) the definition of job expectations.

And Then There Was "Super Dave"

With Cynthia's departure came Dave. "Super Dave" made remarkable progress in his first three months on the job. A record number of new members and sponsors came on board. Dave, heralded as "Hawkley's Marketing Genius," was featured on the local radio and television news programs. He always spoke smoothly and looked like a winner. When interviewed about the key to successful marketing, Dave followed his well-polished formula. First, he cited general, basic marketing principles. Then he concluded with the following sentence, which had become his trademark: "As for the rest, well, it's a certain *Je ne sais quois.*" Super Dave was becoming a local celebrity.

The members of Hawkley's board of directors were beside themselves with delight, certain they'd finally found their man. He had the image, style, and financial results. Based on the number of new members and sponsors, unprecedented profits had been predicted for the first two quarters of Dave's employment. Strangely, after the first three months, despite numerous new members and sponsors, not a single membership fee had been received in those three months. Further investigation revealed that Dave had been recruiting new sponsors and members with his "secret" marketing strategy. Dave's famous *Je ne sais quois* was this: If you join Hawkley, your first year of membership or sponsorship is entirely free, no strings attached. It turned out that Dave was not a marketing specialist at all. He simply gave sponsors and new members an offer they could not refuse: full membership at no cost. What Dave got out of it was what he described as "the best six months of my life. I golfed every day, ate the best food, drank the best drinks, and met the richest people in the city. It was one long celebration. Thanks, Hawkley!" And then Dave would laugh, thinking about the six-month celebration that had cost Hawkley $112,000 in entertaining expenses alone. Super Dave, with a high school education and a false resume, had done very well for himself. The hiring committee (i.e., the board of directors) had not checked any references. They just liked the polished "image" they'd perceived.

Could an MBO system of evaluation have prevented this disaster for Hawkley? Why or why not?

See appendix C for reflections on the cases.

Performance Appraisal Forms: Sample Job Descriptions

Appendix A includes many examples of job descriptions for personnel within sport organizations. They are provided as examples to help you generate job descriptions specific to your organization. Remember that job descriptions flow from careful job analysis. They are completely dependent on the specific organization and the environment and culture that drives the organization. Therefore, the same position in two different contexts could, perhaps even should, have different job descriptions. Those included in this appendix are provided as samples of effective job descriptions. Use them to develop those specific to your organization after completing job analysis for a position. Remember, effective job descriptions are concise, clearly worded guidelines for a job. They explain the work and outline the skill, responsibility, and complexity involved.

- A.1 College/University Athletic Director
- A.2 College/University Head Coach
- A.3 Marketing Manager
- A.4 Sports Information Manager
- A.5 Events Manager
- A.6 High School Coach
- A.7 National Team Coach

A.1   College/University Athletic Director

The athletic director (AD) is responsible for the planning, implementation, administration, coordination, and evaluation of all activities within the Department of Athletics and Recreational Services (DARS). In general, this position demands responsibility and provides authority for conducting DARS programming in an educational context and within the established policies and procedures of the University Senate and Board of Governors. The AD is responsible for the following:

- Development and leadership of the intercollegiate athletic program
- Development and leadership of the campus recreation program
- Maintenance of academic and athletic standards as required by the regulations of the university, regional association, and national or international athletic organizations
- Advisement of the department council, Dean, President, Senate and Board of Governors on policies and procedures for athletics and recreation
- Development and administration of the budget, ensuring that allocations appropriately reflect the department philosophy

- Promotion of liaison and public relations by means of athletics and recreation to the various segments of the university, and with education and government at community, county, provincial or state, national, and international levels
- Advisement to the Appointments Committee on process, selection, appointment, and retention of full- and part-time coaches, recreation supervisors, and program personnel
- Evaluation and recommendation to the appropriate person or committee on matters related to promotions, tenure, renewal, and merit pay
- Evaluation of the athletic and recreation programs and recommendation on additions or deletions
- Communication with the university community and participants regarding the department, university, provincial or state, and national policies and procedures on sport and recreation

Specific responsibilities include the following:

- Preparation and administration of budget and accounting procedures
- Supervision of tendering, procurement, dispensation, and retrieval of equipment and supplies
- Preparation of reports and retention of records
- Supervising publicity and coordination of public relations related to DARS
- Advising on policies and procedures for facilities, equipment, and supplies
- Representing the university at community, school sport, amateur athletic, and recreation organizations
- Preparing and presenting proactive or reactive position papers in cooperation with students, faculty, staff, and administration relating to amateur athletic or recreation developments
- Remaining available to faculty and students for course presentations and research studies related to school sport or amateur/professional athletics and recreation
- Coordinating assignment of participation and special awards
- Enforcing policies and procedures of the department, senate, and board of governors in consort with senior university administration, president, vice-presidents, registrar, deans, directors, and other academic and administrative officers

- Representing the university at league meetings for scheduling, semiannual and annual legislative assembly meetings, special meetings, emergency meetings, and committee meetings
- Retaining sport and recreation in an educational context as each relate to their respective organizations
- Acting as corresponding agent for the university in terms of department philosophy and financial management, and for general inquiries
- Carrying the university's share of workload in league responsibilities on executive, committees, sport leadership, hosting, etc. in the athletic conferences and recreation associations
- Representing the university and its interests at the national association meetings
- Sharing responsibility for the organization and administration of athletics and recreation at the national and international levels as appointed or elected by recreational, national, and international organizations

A.2 College/University Head Coach

Preamble

This position encompasses primary accountability for the direction of day-to-day activities and program development for *[sport and school]*. The incumbent is responsible for adhering to all department and league policies and procedures, and reports directly to the director of athletics.

This position is considered integral to the department as it seeks to fulfill the mission of providing opportunities for participation in highly organized competitive sport to university students.

It is intended that coaches be guided by the following values that are endorsed by all department members and that define our desired organizational climate. Generally these values include a commitment to the following:

1. The pursuit of professional and personal excellence
2. Information sharing
3. Fairness, honesty, and integrity
4. Gender equity within programming
5. Projection of a positive image at work and in the community
6. Academics-before-athletics approach for student-athletes
7. Safety of all program participants

8. Planning in order to *maximize*

(a) direction,

(b) motivation,

(c) instruction,

(d) progress information,

(e) production,

(f) positive experience,

(g) fair play and honorable competition,

(h) variety,

(i) self-determination,

(j) social experience, and

(k) support.

These outcomes will be achieved through the following five categories of specific behaviors, tasks, activities, and responsibilities:

1. Day-to-day coaching
2. Recruiting
3. Athlete and team outcomes
4. Program administration
5. Public relations/professional development

Specific behaviors, tasks, activities, and responsibilities

The coach is responsible for the following:

1. The day-to-day application of coaching as it pertains to . . .

    a. Utilizing current and specific theory and techniques toward optimally training [sport] athletes to reach their fullest potential

    b. Teaching appropriate skills, game tactics, and strategies, while using effective techniques for skill and movement analysis

    c. Making appropriate coaching decisions during competition

    d. Developing a positive interpersonal relationship with athletes and student personnel involved with the program

    e. Developing specific practice and game plans

    f. Motivating, disciplining, and leading athletes toward their highest possible achievements

    g. Developing a positive, professional relationship with game officials, league personnel, and coaching colleagues

    h. Developing a disciplined team in both conduct and appearance, as judged both on and off the court

2. Building the program through recruiting

    a. Establishing a recruiting plan for identifying, contacting, and communicating with top high school athletes in (a) the city and county area, (b) this and other local provinces or states, and (c) other areas of the country with reasonable potential for successful recruiting

b. Bringing potential student-athletes to visit our campus to tour academic and athletic facilities, and meet with both athletic and academic individuals

c. Establishing a public relations link with scholastic and club level [sport] both locally and at the state or provincial level, and if possible nationally, in order to increase the visibility of your program, yourself, and our university

d. Working to achieve a sport-specific profile at all levels via media opportunities, attendance at games wherever possible, volunteer coaching in club programs or clinics, and speaking engagements

e. Working toward the recruitment goal: quality of athlete first, quantity of athletes second

3. Anticipated athlete and team outcomes

a. Improvement over the course of a season, or from previous seasons assessed on a yearly basis

b. Team and individual athlete accomplishments in relation to their potential

c. Participation in the playoffs, or being in the top half of the league

d. Satisfaction of team members

e. Team cohesiveness

f. Athlete-centered approach to coaching

4. Administrative tasks associated with coaching

a. Taking accountability in all financial matters in relation to travel, purchase of equipment, and otherwise

b. Conducting both short- and long-term planning, as related to optimal preparation for the duties of the preseason, season, and postseason

c. Attending league and national meetings

d. Monitoring athlete eligibility and academic standing/progress

e. Completing paper work on time

f. Contributing to the overall atmosphere of the department through establishing positive, team-oriented working relationships with peers

g. Defining an effective competitive schedule within budget constraints

5. Public relations and professional development

   a. Aggressively pursuing a positive relationship with local media

   b. Serving on department and university committees

   c. Conducting summer sports camps (where applicable)

   d. Being involved with professional association (where applicable)

   e. Upgrading education—especially coaching education through attaining coaching certification levels

   f. Becoming and working as a resource person for high school and elementary school coaches (where applicable)

   g. Attaining certification of Technical Course Conductor status and offer technical courses in the local area

A.3   Marketing Manager

The position of marketing manager involves the planning, coordination, and day-to-day operation of activities pertinent to marketing the athletics and recreation programs within this department. The incumbent is responsible for adherence to departmental policy and procedures in all matters pertaining to marketing the programs and must work closely with department colleagues in coaching, program administration, sports information and communication, and event management. The incumbent will provide input and assistance to the athletic director to whom the incumbent directly reports.

The marketing manager is responsible for the following:

- Developing a marketing plan based on pertinent market research and forecasting
- Soliciting, delivering, and servicing sponsorship agreements in both the short and long term
- Organizing, pricing, and managing event advertising
- Developing an overall promotional strategy for the department as a whole
- Conducting ongoing market research pertinent to the athletics and recreation environment
- Developing marketing materials
- Supervising field support
- Closely communicating with other department professionals for the delivery of professional advertisement

- Keeping financial records relative to all aspects of the marketing initiatives
- Building long-term relationships between the department and the business community
- Implementing department philosophy pertaining to equity and the promotion of women's sport
- Implementing department philosophy pertaining to equity and the promotion of recreation and healthy living through the pursuit of leisure activities
- Soliciting marketing partnerships, relationship building, contract negotiation, delivery of contractual obligations, and further servicing of sponsors
- Financial and budget management relative to all marketing initiatives
- Developing and achieving reasonable sponsorship target goals in both cash and contra agreements

A.4   Sports Information Manager

The sports information manager is responsible for media liaison relative to university athletic and recreational programming, the organization and dissemination of athletic event results, and the management and development of all home athletic events. The incumbent will have a keen interest in sport and recreation, and knowledge of the local, provincial or state, and national university sport environment. The incumbent will have the ability to raise the profile of team accomplishments and will be responsible for media liaison as well as the distribution of results and all relevant information to media and affiliated sport organizations. The incumbent will also be responsible for enhancing event management, and coordinating and supervising all aspects of such events; consultation for publications, special awards, Web site development and maintenance, photograph inventory, and record keeping; and department image and public profile building.

Specific accountabilities include the following:

1. Managing budget for sport information, advertising, promotions, and home events
2. Leading athletics event management and hosting, including the supervision of the full-time, part-time, and student employees for the delivery of home events, sports reporting, and advertising

3. Establishing, writing, and implementing annual marketing plans to promote home game events with the express purpose of increasing attendance

4. Creating liaisons with sport coaches

5. Producing game announcement packages

6. Linking with and supervising the sports photographer

7. Conducting all sport media relations, sport announcing, and sport reporting of events

8. Working with marketing manager

9. Keeping event result statistics and records

10. Delivering championship events

11. Using current technology and sport publications, and maintaining knowledge of sport delivery systems

Work schedule: flexible, to account for the coverage of evening and weekend events and media time lines.

A.5   Events Manager

Reporting to the AD, the events manager is responsible for the delivery of all aspects of approximately 100 athletic events held on campus during the academic year.

Specific duties include the following:

1. Hire, supervise, and evaluate all home event workers.

2. Ensure an appropriate delivery of the national anthem(s).

3. Develop a comprehensive home event plan.

4. Assist with the promotion and publicity of all home events.

5. Plan and deliver all special and regular promotion activities surrounding home events.

6. Work with the sports information manager for media, television, and game announcement activities.

7. Ensure the electronic compilation of statistics.

8. Ensure proper event facility setup and cleanliness.

9. Ensure adequate security.

10. Manage all aspects of home event workers' assignment of activities and work with coaches, media, and game officials.

11. During the summer months, develop specific operational plans for event management and staffing for the coming year in liaison with marketing and facility personnel.

A.6 High School Coach

Position title: head coach

Report to: physical education/athletic director.

Responsible for the following:

1. Diligently creating a safe sport environment for play, practice, travel, and all other matters associated with the school team.
2. Planning and preparing for the preseason, season, and postseason of play.
3. Scheduling and preparing travel arrangements.
4. Planning and effective teaching of the sport during practice, specific to the age group involved.
5. Communicating with and motivating athletes.
6. Inculcating principles of fair play and honorable competition, consistent with the philosophy for all school sport teams.
7. Developing game plans.
8. Purchasing, storing, and taking inventory of equipment.
9. Making appropriate coaching decisions during games.
10. Developing a positive and supportive media relationship.
11. Communicating with parents.
12. Ensuring a positive, professional relationship with game officials, league personnel, and coaching colleagues.
13. Hiring, supervising, and effectively using assistant coaches.
14. Being punctual and professional in handling all administrative functions.
15. Leading by example.

A.7 National Team Coach

The national XYZ coach is accountable for the development of athletes into a team capable of achieving world-class performances while also contributing to the physical, psychological, and social development of individual athletes. The coach is responsible for planning, organizing, implementing, and controlling a comprehensive competition, training, and monitoring program. Consistent improvement in performance by the nation's athletes within the financial constraints imposed by the association is an important measure of success. It is expected that the coach will have a thorough understanding of the scientific principles of training. The coach is responsible for communication with provincial or state and university coaches, and is expected to take a prominent role for the future development of sport XYZ within the country. The position involves a high degree of public visibility, and it is expected that the coach will represent the association in a positive fashion at all times.

Specific accountabilities include the following:

1. Athlete development and preparation

   1.1 Establish plans for the physiological, psychological, technical, and tactical components of the program

   1.2 Identify clear objectives for achievement in training and competition

   (and so on . . .)

2. Program planning

   2.1 In collaboration with assistant coaches, establish the quadrennial plan, objectives, and yearly components of the plan, toward reaching determined performance objectives

   2.2 Design and communicate an athlete selection system

   (and so on . . .)

3. Team management

   3.1 Direct, supervise, and evaluate all program support staff

   3.2 Ensure that team equipment and clothing are used in a manner consistent with sponsor and other contractual obligations

   (and so on . . .)

4. Personnel management

   4.1 Establish expectations for standards of behavior for all personnel involved with the program

   4.2 Direct, supervise, and evaluate assistant coaches

   (and so on . . .)

5. Association management

5.1 Attend association meetings and prepare reports and presentations as required

5.2 Promote the program to the membership, sponsors, and public (and so on . . .)

Adapted from Sport Canada (1987).

A.8 Travel Manager

The incumbent will be responsible for all components of department travel including, but not limited to, the following:

1. Communicate with coaches regarding team travel schedules, departure and arrival time, and modes of transportation.
2. Work with assistant AD regarding team complements, confirmation of schedules, modes of transportation, and departure and arrival times.
3. Request tenders for ground transportation and hotel accommodations for team travel.
4. Maintain travel planner for each trip, recording details of type of transportation and company confirmed, amount of meal allowance required, confirmation of accommodations, etc.
5. Complete check requisitions for meal allowances for each trip.
6. Post details of a team's travel for equipment technicians.
7. Prepare a coach's package outlining all details of each trip, such as type of ground transportation, meal allotment, expense report.
8. Reconfirm arrangements with transportation companies and hotels for all trips before the week's travel.
9. Compare coaches' expense reports with travel planner.
10. Mail refunds, invoices, claims, and expense reports to finance department immediately following each trip.
11. Summarize travel expenses for each team at the completion of a team's season.
12. Make arrangements for travel for department personnel.
13. Keep accurate and up-to-date files on accommodations in cities normally visited by university teams or department personnel.
14. Keep accurate and up-to-date files for all aspects of travel arranged in a given year.

A.9   Assistant Athletic Director

The position of assistant AD encompasses primary responsibility for the day-to-day operation of the intercollegiate athletic program. The incumbent is responsible for adherence to department and league policy and procedures. The assistant AD will provide input and assistance to the AD on all requested matters and will have responsibility for duties as assigned by the AD in addition to those listed here.

Primary accountabilities include the following:

- Supervision of tendering, procurement, dispensation, and retrieval of equipment and supplies
- Preparation of practice, exhibition, and league schedules, and assurance of fulfillment of game commitments and contracts
- Preparation of eligibility lists and enforcement of academic requirements of the university and league organizations
- Coordination of the efforts of coaches, managers, and athletes in the planning, operation, and evaluation of the sports programs
- Preparation of reports and retention of records
- Representation of the university at community, school sport, and amateur athletic organizations
- Hosting of incoming teams for competition on the university campus
- Completion of studies and surveys as requested and required

Supervision

- Student interns—15
- Program personnel for women's teams—16
- Coaching staff for women's teams—29

Work schedule: flexibility is incorporated in the schedule to cover events scheduled on weekends and in the evening.

Discretion allowed: changes to budgetary allocations and strategies for the management of public relations must be discussed with the AD.

A.10   Recreation Director

Preamble

The campus recreation director is responsible for the planning, delivery, and evaluation of the campus and community recreation program. The program is divided into two sections with each section containing four core areas. Each core area offers a wide variety of leagues, activities, and classes for several campus and community constituents.

Intramural component

1. Men's program core
2. Women's program core
3. Coed program core
4. Special events

Service component

5. Aquatics program core
6. Children's program core
7. Professional development core
8. Fitness and dance core

Responsible to the director of athletics and recreational services, the recreation director is accountable for the following duties:

1. Planning, promotion, delivery, and evaluation of a comprehensive recreational program designed to meet the recreational needs of university students, staff, faculty, alumni, and community
2. Developing and administering the budget, ensuring that allocations appropriately reflect departmental and school philosophy, as well as meet the standards for accounting procedures as defined by the finance department
3. Recruiting, training, supervising, and evaluating student managers (25), office workers (5), referees (35), and instructors (40) employed by the program
4. Supervising the tendering, procurement, dispensation, and retrieval of equipment and supplies for the recreation program
5. Supervising publicity and coordination of public relations related to the Campus Recreation program
6. Cooperating with the other program and facility administrators in the integration of all programming
7. Advising on policies and procedures for facilities, equipment, and supplies
8. Maintaining a high profile with municipal, provincial or state, and national associations that promote recreational sports programming and healthy lifestyles
9. Developing professionally through attendance at related conferences, workshops, and clinics

A.11   Assistant Recreation Director

The campus recreation assistant is responsible to the campus recreation director and chair of the department of athletics and recreational services. The incumbent is specifically responsible for the following areas:

1. Registration coordination
   - Supervise and organize early registration on campus
   - Complete, maintain, and distribute class registration lists
   - Compile a term-end budget report
   - Schedule and supervise office staff
   - Compose a monthly newsletter for recreation staff
   - Maintain the office in a neat and orderly manner
2. Intramural coordination
   - Supervise and evaluate supervisors, sport managers, and officials
   - Coordinate the intramural entry and captain's meeting
   - Supervise intramural staff training and meetings
   - Follow up on occurrences and accidents
   - Ensure the management of risk for all intramural activities
   - Work with sponsors
   - Maintain a current equipment inventory
   - Assist in the upkeep of the Intramural Championship Display Board and awards
3. Special event coordination
   - Assist with all special events, such as Frosh week, Health Fair, Headstart, March Break, Sport Tournaments, Natural High events, and year-end Appreciation Night
   - Assist with the coordination of volunteers
   - Act as a liaison with campus departments, such as student societies, residences, and health services
   - Plan, supervise, and ensure the development of promotional material for the advancement of campus recreation
4. Program evaluation
   - Coordinate program evaluation for all areas of campus recreation
   - Provide a summary of evaluation results for each program area
   - Review evaluations and make recommendations to the recreation director

A.12   Athletics Business Manager

Reporting to the AD, the business manager is responsible for the maintenance of all financial records, the completion of financial transactions, financial forecasting, budget development, event management finances, and all other matters relative to the financial accountability of the department of athletics and recreational services.

Specific duties include the following:

1. Prepare and process all requests for check requisitions.
2. Research equipment suppliers and obtain quotes for equipment purchases.
3. Provide weekly summaries of budget activities to cost center signing authorities.
4. Prepare and process all purchase requisitions.
5. Manage all event floats and gate accounts, and prepare all bank deposits.
6. Maintain current spread sheets for all budgets.
7. Advise AD on matters of financial management.
8. Ensure deadlines for payment are achieved.
9. Pay all department invoices.
10. Ensure all athletic and campus recreation fees are collected in a timely manner.
11. Develop all department financial reports.
12. Prepare and manage all student payroll activities.
13. Manage all other bookkeeping and accounting functions for the department.

A.13 Recruiting Coach

Reporting to the assistant AD, the recruiting coach is responsible for the development of a comprehensive recruiting plan and recruitment network of alumni and volunteers to assist with recruiting in women's and men's varsity basketball, volleyball, soccer, and ice hockey. The incumbent will be responsible to the head coaches in the sports listed here and will take primary responsibility for the identification of new out-of-state athletic talent to assist the team's coaching staff in their recruitment efforts. It is accepted that local and state recruitment is the sole responsibility of the sport-specific coaching staff.

Specific duties include the following:

1. Prepare a recruitment and talent identification travel plan for optimal coverage of out-of-state talent identification.

2. Meet bimonthly with the head coach to discuss upcoming recruitment initiatives and discuss identified talent and contact information.

3. Keep a data base of all identified talent, updated with contact information, academic interests, academic background, and other pertinent information.

4. Develop and maintain strong working relationship with high school and club-level coaches around the country.

5. Advocate on behalf of all academic and athletic programs at the college.

6. Coordinate the collection of talent videotape and other competitive information for head and assistant coaches.

7. Remain knowledgeable and current in the policies, procedures, and trends of college academic and athletic programming, especially as these pertain to the sports in which the incumbent is charged with the identification of talent.

8. Ensure follow-up on all questions and requests for information received from potential recruits, their coaches, or their families.

9. Develop and promote a recruitment Web site related to the incumbent's own recruitment efforts.

10. Ensure an awareness of the best practices of the recruiting efforts of competitors.

A.14   Paid College Assistant Coach

The assistant coach reports directly to the head coach of the program, while owing responsibility to the AD and the policies and procedures of the college at large. The duties attached to this position might change respecting the different pressure points inherent to an athletic season, but will normally include some or all of the following:

1. Supervising statisticians, managers, and graduate-level assistants

2. Ensuring that all equipment is set up, retrieved, stored, and inventoried in an efficient and timely manner

3. Videotaping breakdown of opponents

4. Overseeing practice warm-ups

5. Providing input on practice planning as requested by the head coach

6. Providing input in game analysis as requested by the head coach

7. Teaching as assigned by the head coach

8. Contributing to team motivation and communication

9. Checking travel plans and authorizing travel logistics

10. Completing other duties as assigned

A.15 Volunteer Coach

The coach is responsible for the following:

1. Directing the team in all scheduled practices

2. Developing team strategy, training regime, and competitive philosophy

3. Motivating, leading, and developing athletes to learn, develop as competitors, and maintain a love for sport

4. Ensuring the team abides by rules and is disciplined

5. Developing competitive schedules when requested to do so

6. Behaving according to the highest professional standards of conduct, and maintaining courteous interactions with officials, parents, opposing coaches, and the media

7. Maintaining health records and injury reports for all occurrences of injury

8. Submitting travel itineraries to the club director at least one week before travel

9. Conducting regular facility safety audits before competing at home and on the road

10. Attending to the requests of club management in a timely, efficient manner

The coach is responsible to the board of directors of the athletic club.

The coach is expected to receive board approval for all financial matters associated with the team.

A.16 Strength and Conditioning Coach

The strength and conditioning coach reports directly to the assistant AD while maintaining close contact with the varsity coaching staff. The main responsibility of this position is to assist coaches and individual athletes with the development of effective strength and conditioning programs in the pursuit of a specific training goal. The job incumbent will be responsible for the following:

1. Individual and team training sessions
2. Developing a data base of training information, accessible to all varsity program participants
3. Keeping detailed records of prescribed training
4. Helping coaches and athletes to set appropriate conditioning goals throughout a season or several seasons
5. Helping coaches and athletes to monitor conditioning gains throughout a season
6. Ensuring the safety of the strength and conditioning training environment
7. Promoting a drug-free training environment and method
8. Developing and maintaining a training resource library for varsity sport participants
9. Communicating training information pertinent to injury status to athletic therapy
10. Educating athletes and coaches about safe strength training

A.17   Athletic Trainer

The athletic trainer is responsible for the management of the athletic injuries clinic, the student personnel assigned to teams who work within the clinic, and the treatment of athletic injuries for all varsity athletic teams. The trainer reports to the AD and is accountable for all matters relating to the administration and care of injuries for the athletic program. The incumbent must be a fully certified Athletic Trainer and possess related academic qualifications at a minimal undergraduate level. The incumbent will ensure that the clinic is a clean, welcoming, and professional environment in which athletes seek injury-related assistance. The position requires leadership for the entire sport therapy mission, and specifically involves the examination, prescription of first-aid treatment, short- and long-term rehabilitation of injury, referral to other appropriate care, and prevention of injury. The mandate of the athletic injuries clinic is to help athletes return to competition following injury quickly and safely; to avoid the aggravation of major injuries or emergencies, or chronic injury situations; to minimize the possibility of injury; to provide emergency first aid; and to educate student trainers, athletes, and coaches in the care and prevention of athletic injuries.

Specific duties include the following:

1. Managing the clinic
2. Diagnosing athletes' injuries
3. Rehabilitating athletes' injuries
4. Referring athletes with injuries needing attention from a medical doctor
5. Purchasing of supplies
6. Recruiting, training, and supervision of student trainers
7. Developing a training manual
8. Providing first-aid treatment
9. Educating athletes for the prevention of injuries
10. Inventorying supplies
11. Providing on-site coverage of home games

A.18 Recreational Sport Program Supervisor

A. Employee supervision
   - Train, supervise, and lead all students employed as supervisors, sport managers, and officials.
   - Organize training clinics for sport managers and officials before the commencement of the season.
   - Monitor payroll sheets to ensure that employees are paid accurately and on time.
   - Evaluate student supervisors' performance.

B. Organization of sports program
   - Coordinate all aspects of team registration, and ensure the communication of schedules, rules, and regulations.
   - Ensure functional, safe equipment for each event and retrieval of equipment after the event.
   - Chair the discipline and appeals committee.

C. Publicity
   - Develop and distribute announcement flyers, banners, and posters to advertise the leagues.
   - Submit weekly standings and stories, along with photographs, to the newspaper.

D. Administration
  - Attend weekly staff meetings and assist sport managers with the organization.

A.19   Aquatic Coordinator

The aquatic coordinator is the primary individual responsible for pool services and facilities. Reporting to the director of facility operations, the coordinator must hire, supervise, and schedule approximately 100 lifeguards to ensure the supervision of 105 hours of open pool time within a given week. This individual will prepare and maintain an up-to-date lifeguard training manual, and will ensure the full training of lifeguards to ensure safe operating principles for the pool facility. Regular staff meetings will be conducted. Consistent monitoring of lifeguard certification and employee evaluation is required.

The aquatic coordinator is also accountable for the safe operation of the pool from a technical point of view, with respect to chemical purchase, storage, and use, along with monitoring the heating, water and air exchange, and sanitation for the pool and locker room areas.

The aquatic coordinator must also contribute to the overall management of the fitness facility, helping to plan, organize, lead, and evaluate both personnel and programs from a global organizational perspective. The position involves some weekend, evening, and on-call duty.

A.20   Equipment Manager

Reporting to the services coordinator, the equipment manager is accountable for all aspects of athletic equipment management for all programs run within the facility. Specific responsibilities include:

  a. Equipment inventory and control: conduct computerized cataloging and inventory
  b. Locker control: issue rental lockers and collection of fees
  c. Receiving: receive and inspect all new equipment, and notify requisitioners
  d. Equipment repair: repair, modify, and/or maintain all athletic equipment
  e. Equipment issue: comply with requests for the issuance of all equipment

f. Equipment retrieval: conduct all retrieval, adjustment, and removal of facility setups

g. Key control: sign in and sign out keys to rooms and storage

h. Audiovisual: comply with requests for audiovisual equipment

i. Miscellaneous: oversee student supervision, laundry, public relations, risk management

A.21 Sport Camp Instructor

The sport camp instructor's responsibilities include the following:

1. Design and distribute camp registration flyers and posters.

2. Hire staff to ensure the effective registration of participants, along with the appropriate teaching of skills via a progression of drill and scrimmage settings.

3. Prepare and instruct safe, enjoyable, and effective sport-specific camps, appropriate to the level and age group of the participants.

4. Requisition the necessary equipment, and ensure the setup and removal of equipment within the facility no later than 8:30 A.M. and 5:00 P.M.

5. Ensure the supervision of participants at all times from 9 A.M. to 4 P.M., at a ratio of no greater than one supervisor to ten participants.

6. Assign camp leaders to teaching stations and communicate minimal teaching standards.

7. Ensure that parental and participant consent forms are on file for each camp participant.

8. Complete payroll sheets for staff, and conduct evaluation of all staff members at the conclusion of the program.

9. Generate feedback report cards for each camp participant to provide encouragement for youngsters to continue practicing sport.

10. Design and order camp awards, and conduct the awards ceremony at the end of the camp during the Awards and Parents Appreciation Ceremony.

A.22 Academic Counselor

Each academic counselor is responsible for the supervision and communication of academic priorities for one varsity team. The incumbent is specifically responsible for the following areas:

1. Evening study hall
   - Venue
   - Organization
   - Supervision
   - Study skills training session
   - Time management training session
   - Attendance
2. Grade supervision
   - Develop grade files from reports submitted by each athlete
   - Keep a computerized data base
   - Conduct trend analysis and problem identification
   - Follow up after all evaluations (papers, tests, etc.)
   - Hold confidential discussions with individual athletes
3. Assignment of study partners and tutors
   - Assign athletes (via year and course work) to study partners or groups
   - Provide senior student tutors to high-risk students
   - Assign tutors to identified underachieving students
4. Communication to coaching staff
   - Ensure that the coaching staff is supportive of academic initiatives
   - Communicate academic problems to head coach
   - Help manage year-end academic achievement awards with coaches

A.23   High School Athletic Director

Department of Physical Education
   Job title: Athletic Director
   Date of last update:
   Accountable to: high school principal
   Job purpose: Management of the interscholastic sports program, with specific responsibility for organization, planning, evaluation, leadership, and internal and external relations
   Manages: 20 varsity sport activities and associated coaching staff.
   Specific responsibilities:

1. Organization: it is expected that the incumbent will have good overall knowledge of school sports and strong organizational skills. The

incumbent will be responsible for organizing or supervising the coach's organization of all aspects of team travel; purchase of equipment; inventory and storage of equipment; the management of home games, including securing major and minor officials; and training and scheduling student workers. The incumbent will ensure that all aspects of the high school sports program comply with the standards set by the league of play and the rules governing the individual sport, especially as they pertain to student-athlete eligibility for competition.

2. Planning: the AD will ensure proper planning for all sports by outlining or supervising the planning of competitive schedules, practice schedules, facility scheduling, and the definition of equitable hosting parameters. The incumbent will also be responsible for budget planning, staffing arrangements, the efficient use of personnel, and the development of common rules policy.

3. Evaluation: the AD will ensure the training, supervision, and appraisal of all staff; will evaluate or define a procedure for evaluating the overall sports program; will ensure compliance to rules of athlete eligibility; and will evaluate all programs, policies, facilities, and staff actions to ensure the safety of all participants and to strategically manage the inherent risk associated with sport.

4. Leadership: the AD will provide overall leadership in all matters pertaining to the interscholastic sports program and ensure that common practices align with school philosophy. Such policy development should include, but not be limited to: equitable distribution of programming and resources for boys' and girls' sport; management of discipline in accordance with school policy; all matters related to fund raising; and the assurance of ethical decision making and support for an environment of fair play.

5. External and internal relations: the AD is expected to work with external partners such as parents, the media, officials from other schools, and the league within which they operate. The AD is also expected to manage the department internally to ensure proper communication, compliance to rules, and the fair and equitable distribution of resources. The internal environment will be enhanced by the stellar professional conduct of the AD and by the AD's ability to develop effective working relationships, commitment, and management skills regarding efficiency.

Sample Performance Appraisal Forms and Checklists

Appendix B provides many sample forms and checklists that will enable you to engage the management by objectives performance appraisal procedure outlined within this book. It is recommended that you might use these forms as is or convert them to reflect your situation more appropriately. Each can be edited to include your organization's logo and header, numbered as appropriate, and then saved in your word processor.

B.1 MBO Annual Checklist for Manager

Employee Name:_____

Position:_____

Year in Cycle: 1   2   3   Date: _____

Task	**Date Accomplished**
❏ Evaluation criteria established	_____
❏ Goals meeting #1 date confirmed	_____
❏ Goals meeting #1 discussion prepared	_____
❏ Goals meeting	_____
❏ Documentation up to date	_____
❏ Collect performance information	_____
	_____
	_____
	_____
❏ Schedule and conduct progress meeting	_____
❏ Documentation up to date	_____
❏ Collect performance information	_____
❏ Collect self, peer, subordinate ratings	_____
❏ Collate information and prepare appraisal	_____
	_____
	_____
	_____
	_____
❏ Schedule and conduct year-end meeting	_____
❏ Sign-off on written appraisal	_____
❏ File paper work	_____

B.2   MBO Data Diary Form

Employee Name:_____

Position:_____

Year in Cycle: 1   2   3   Date: _____

Date:_____   **Setting:**_____

Notes:

Other information appended?   Yes ❏   No ❏

Required follow-up:

B.3   Goal Setting Meeting Form

Employee Name:_____

Position:_____

Year in Cycle: 1   2   3   Date: _____

Goal:

Action plan:

Goal priority # _____
_____

Goal:

Action plan:

Goal priority # _____
_____

Goal:

Action plan:

Goal priority # _____
_____

Page _____ of _____

B.4 Coach Evaluation Form: College/University Example

Employee Name:_____

Sport: _____

Year in Cycle: 1   2   3   Date: _____

Scale: 5 = Distinguished; 4 = Superior; 3 = Competent; 2 = Fair; 1 = Marginal

Day-to-day application of coaching:	**Circle one**
1. Communicating with athletes	1 2 3 4 5
2. Applying sport knowledge	1 2 3 4 5
3. Motivating athletes to higher achievement	1 2 3 4 5
4. Utilizing game tactics and strategies	1 2 3 4 5
5. Applying conditioning principles	1 2 3 4 5
6. Teaching techniques during practice	1 2 3 4 5
7. Coaching decisions during competition	1 2 3 4 5
8. Conducting practice sessions	1 2 3 4 5
9. Planning for segments of yearly season	1 2 3 4 5
10. Developing game plans	1 2 3 4 5

Average:_____

Building the sport program:	
11. Making recruiting contacts	1 2 3 4 5
12. Scouting opponents	1 2 3 4 5
13. Establishing a recruiting plan	1 2 3 4 5
14. Maintaining and using statistics	1 2 3 4 5
15. Recruiting a specific number of athletes	1 2 3 4 5
16. Recruiting quality athletes	1 2 3 4 5

Average:_____

(continued)

B.4 Coach Evaluation Form: College/University Example

Managing the sport program:

17. Monitoring athlete eligibility	1 2 3 4 5
18. Adhering to budget	1 2 3 4 5
19. Adhering to rules and regulations	1 2 3 4 5
20. Working relationships with department staff	1 2 3 4 5
21. Purchase of equipment	1 2 3 4 5
22. Being on time with paper work	1 2 3 4 5
23. Working relationships with peer coaches	1 2 3 4 5
24. Complying with institution's philosophy	1 2 3 4 5

Average:_____

Public relations:

25. Working with high school coaches	1 2 3 4 5
26. Conducting summer sports camps	1 2 3 4 5
27. Working relationships with parents	1 2 3 4 5
28. Involvement with professional association	1 2 3 4 5
29. Presenting at player/coaching clinics	1 2 3 4 5

Average:_____

Team/athlete results:

30. Team win-loss record	1 2 3 4 5
31. Making the playoffs	1 2 3 4 5
32. Improvement from previous season	1 2 3 4 5
33. Improvement over current season	1 2 3 4 5
34. Performance of individual athlete(s)	1 2 3 4 5

Average:_____

Outcomes of coaching personal to the coach:

35. Receiving coaching awards	1 2 3 4 5
36. Writing for publication	1 2 3 4 5
37. Invited public appearances	1 2 3 4 5
38. Speaking engagements	1 2 3 4 5
39. Upgrading coach's certification	1 2 3 4 5

Average:_____

Overall average score: _____

Comments:

Note: The criteria listed in this form are examples. They must be tailored to the specific job under evaluation.

B.5 Coach Evaluation Form: High School Example

Employee Name:_____

Sport: _____

Year in Cycle: 1 2 3   Date: _____

Scale: 5 = Excellent; 4 = Good; 3 = Average; 2 = Need improvement;
                 1 = Unacceptable

Coaching ability: **Circle one**

1. Knowledge of sport and sport rules   1 2 3 4 5

2. Ability to teach the sport   1 2 3 4 5

3. Appropriate to age group and situation   1 2 3 4 5

4. Use of recent concepts in sport and coaching   1 2 3 4 5

5. Makes safety of participants a top priority   1 2 3 4 5

6. Makes maximum use of practice time   1 2 3 4 5

7. Prepares the team physically (conditioning)   1 2 3 4 5

8. Prepares the team mentally (scouting, motivation) 1 2 3 4 5

9. Prepares the team tactically (game planning)   1 2 3 4 5

10. Makes good use of assistant coaches   1 2 3 4 5

11. Treats players with respect, honesty, and courtesy 1 2 3 4 5

12. Acts to prevent, care for, and follow up   1 2 3 4 5
    on athletic injuries

Philosophy:

13. Coaching aligns with the philosophy of the school 1 2 3 4 5

14. Has team discipline and control, in all situations 1 2 3 4 5

15. Is punctual and demands punctuality   1 2 3 4 5

16. Is fair, tolerant, and patient with athletes   1 2 3 4 5

17. Refrains from abusive or foul language   1 2 3 4 5

18. Conducts him/herself calmly and professionally   1 2 3 4 5

19. Abides by all policies and procedures   1 2 3 4 5

Management:

20. Keeps AD informed of major problems/decisions   1 2 3 4 5

21. Issues, cares for, and inventories equipment   1 2 3 4 5

22. Keeps accurate records   1 2 3 4 5

23. Organizes and plans for the season   1 2 3 4 5

24. Communicates with other athletic staff members   1 2 3 4 5

25. Attends to public relations issues appropriately   1 2 3 4 5

26. Able to anticipate problems and define solutions   1 2 3 4 5

Other requirements:

27. Dresses appropriately for practices and games   1 2 3 4 5

28. Sets an example for athletes   1 2 3 4 5

29. Contributes to the administration of the league   1 2 3 4 5

30. Looks for ways to improve the program   1 2 3 4 5

Overall average score: _____

Comments:

Note: The criteria listed in this form are examples. They must be tailored to the specific job under evaluation.

B.6 Administrator Evaluation Form: College/University Example

Employee Name:_____

Position:_____

Year in Cycle: 1   2   3   N/A   Date: _____

Scale: 5 = Outstanding;   4 = Good;   3 = Average;
             2 = Below average;   1 = Incompetent

Planning: Circle one

1. Effectively plans on the short term (yearly)   1   2   3   4   5

2. Effectively plans on the longer term (3-5 years)   1   2   3   4   5

3. Ability to set specific goals   1   2   3   4   5

4. Capacity to define a personnel plan   1   2   3   4   5

5. Plans in accord with the unit's mission   1   2   3   4   5

6. Ability to plan via financial analysis   1   2   3   4   5

7. Makes good decisions based on planning   1   2   3   4   5

Organizing:

8. Uses time effectively   1   2   3   4   5

9. Runs productive meetings   1   2   3   4   5

10. Effectively stages home events   1   2   3   4   5

11. Manages athlete eligibility error-free   1   2   3   4   5

12. Proficiently develops competitive schedules   1   2   3   4   5

13. Is effective in policy development   1   2   3   4 ·5

14. Is effective in project management   1   2   3   4   5

15. Is able to delegate appropriately   1   2   3   4   5

16. Is able to create appropriate priorities   1   2   3   4   5

Leading:

17. Communicates effectively within the unit   1   2   3   4   5

18. Communicates effectively within organization   1   2   3   4   5

19. Works to motivate employees   1   2   3   4   5

20. Has good people skills   1   2   3   4   5

21. Compels others to follow his/her lead   1   2   3   4   5

22. Has a vision   1   2   3   4   5

Evaluating:

23. Manages personnel evaluation effectively   1   2   3   4   5

24. Manages program evaluation effectively   1   2   3   4   5

25. Has defined a performance management system   1   2   3   4   5

26. Is attuned to activities of all employees   1   2   3   4   5

Creating a positive work environment:

27. Is available to employees   1   2   3   4   5

28. Is supportive of employees   1   2   3   4   5

29. Advocates well on behalf of the unit   1   2   3   4   5

30. Is a builder of relationships and coalitions   1   2   3   4   5

31. Has developed positive relationships with the media   1   2   3   4   5

32. Has developed positive relationships with alumni   1   2   3   4   5

Other:

33. Is attuned to risk management   1   2   3   4   5

34. Is punctual and demands punctuality   1   2   3   4   5

35. Is fiscally responsible   1   2   3   4   5

36. Is task-oriented and able to accomplish goals   1   2   3   4   5

37. Contributes to league committees   1   2   3   4   5

38. Conducts him/herself professionally at all times   1   2   3   4   5

Overall average score: _____

Comments:

Note: The criteria listed in this form are examples. They must be tailored to the specific job under evaluation.

B.7 Self-Evaluation Form: College Coach Example

This self-assessment form will help you to participate in your performance appraisal to create a plan for your continued career development. The following questions will help you assess your own performance during the evaluation period. Please write your answers to the following questions and make comments on the assessment criteria. Feel free to add any other thoughts that can help me understand your work environment, concerns, and priorities. Please provide me with a copy of this worksheet by _____ in preparation for our meeting on _____.

1. What do you consider to be your most important accomplishments over the evaluation period?

2. What do you need to do to improve your performance? How can this be facilitated, and how can I help?

3. Comment on any areas of your job that you feel unclear on, or areas that represent problem areas or constant irritations.

4. Please list any special accomplishments, awards, or recognitions that I should be aware of.

5. Comment specifically on any of the individual criteria upon which coaching is evaluated and which you feel represent (a) a major accomplishment area for you, and (b) an area in need of improvement (the coaching evaluation form with individual criteria is attached).

6. Please feel free to list any other comments or questions not covered here that may have affected your job performance during the evaluation period.

Thank you! I look forward to our meeting on _____.

Signed: _____ Date: _____

B.8 Peer Evaluation Form: College Coach Example

In an attempt to gather information relative to the performance of _____ over the past year, I would appreciate your response to the following questions. Your input will be held in the strictest confidence, and only trends of performance concerns from several sources will be discussed with the job incumbent. Please provide examples whenever possible, and return this questionnaire no later than _____. Thank you!

1. What do you consider to be the strengths of this coach?

2. What areas of his/her coaching are in need of improvement? How can this improvement be facilitated?

3. Please comment specifically on any of the individual criteria upon which coaching is evaluated, and which you feel represent major accomplishments or areas in need of improvement (the coaching evaluation form with individual criteria is attached).

4. Please feel free to list any other comments or questions not covered here that may have affected this coach's job performance over the past year.

B.9   Student-Athlete Rating of Coaching: Example Form

Coach's Name:_____

Sport:_____

Years on Team: 1   2   3   4   5   Date:_____

Scale: 5 = Strongly agree;   4 = Agree;   3 = Neither agree nor disagree;
                    2 = Disagree;   1 = Strongly disagree

                                                                                    Circle one

1. The coach is very knowledgeable of the technical   1   2   3   4   5
    aspects of the sport.

2. The coach was well prepared for practices.   1   2   3   4   5

3. The coach was effective in communicating with me. 1   2   3   4   5

4. The coach was effective in motivating me to   1   2   3   4   5
    perform to my optimal level.

5. The coach instilled competitive spirit within   1   2   3   4   5
    team members.

6. The coach instilled good sporting values within   1   2   3   4   5
    team members.

7. The coach was a positive role model for me.   1   2   3   4   5

8. I found the experience to be challenging.   1   2   3   4   5

(continued)

(continued)

B.9 Student-Athlete Rating of Coaching: Example Form

9. The coach helped us to succeed as athletes. 1 2 3 4 5

10. The coach emphasized the importance of succeeding as students. 1 2 3 4 5

11. The coach helped me balance academic and athletic priorities appropriately. 1 2 3 4 5

12. The coach emphasized the importance of treating officials with respect. 1 2 3 4 5

13. The coach possesses good public speaking skills. 1 2 3 4 5

14. The coach presents a positive public image. 1 2 3 4 5

15. The coach created good rapport with the athletes. 1 2 3 4 5

16. The coach has developed a strong overall program. 1 2 3 4 5

17. The program has definitely increased my knowledge in the sport. 1 2 3 4 5

18. The program has definitely increased my competence in the sport. 1 2 3 4 5

19. I would recommend this experience to others. 1 2 3 4 5

20. Overall, the coaching of this team was very effective. 1 2 3 4 5

Overall average score: _____

Comments:

Note: The criteria listed in this form are examples. They must be tailored to the specific job under evaluation.

B.10 Student-Athlete Rating of Athletic Trainer: Example Form

Trainer's Name: _____   Date: _____

Your Sport:_____   Years on Team: 1 2 3 4 5

Approximate Number of Contacts With Trainer: _____

Scale: 5 = Strongly agree;   4 = Agree;   3 = Neither agree nor disagree;
             2 = Disagree;   1 = Strongly disagree

Evaluative items: **Circle one**

1. Overall, the treatment I received in the clinic   1 2 3 4 5
   was very helpful.

2. The trainer was very knowledgeable about my injury. 1 2 3 4 5

3. The trainer was very knowledgeable about my   1 2 3 4 5
   treatment.

4. The trainer was organized for appointments.   1 2 3 4 5

5. The trainer was effective in communicating with me. 1 2 3 4 5

6. The trainer was effective in motivating me to   1 2 3 4 5
   perform all treatments.

7. The trainer conducted him/herself professionally.   1 2 3 4 5

Clinic items:

8. Overall, my involvement with the clinic was   1 2 3 4 5
   a positive experience.

9. I found the atmosphere of the clinic to be   1 2 3 4 5
   professional.

10. The clinic has excellent equipment.   1 2 3 4 5

11. All necessary services are offered by the clinic.   1 2 3 4 5

12. I would recommend this clinic to others.   1 2 3 4 5

(continued)

(continued)

B.10 Student-Athlete Rating of Athletic Trainer: Example Form

Comments:

Note: The criteria listed in this form are examples. They must be tailored to the specific job under evaluation.

B.11 Committee Appraisal (Three-Year) Form: Coach Example

Employee Name:_____

Sport: _____

Present Rank: _____ Original Appointment Date:_____

Department:_____

Date:_____

Recommendation:

(Circle one)   Renewal of contract   Nonrenewal of contract

For _____ year term

and/or

Promotion   From rank _____ to_____

Since the last evaluation period, please list additional qualifications/ accomplishments as per the sections below, and append the full Curriculum Vitae:

1. Additional education/certification:

2. Additional coaching experience:

3. Coaching awards/honors:

4. Coaching record:

5. Team/athlete improvement:

6. Invited public appearances/speeches:

7. Coaching clinics conducted:

8. Athlete academic statistics:

9. Recruitment achievements:

10. Fund raising achievements:

11. Published works:

12. Student-athlete ratings of coaching:

13. Contributions to the department (i.e., committee work):

(continued)

(continued)

B.11 Committee Appraisal (Three-Year) Form: Coach Example

14. Contributions to the university:

15. Contributions to the outside community:

16. Rating of coaching over three-year period:

Scale: 5 = Distinguished;   4 = Superior;   3 = Competent;   2 = Fair;
1 = Marginal

Day-to-day application of coaching: **Circle one**

1. Communicating with athletes   1   2   3   4   5

2. Applying sport knowledge   1   2   3   4   5

3. Motivating athletes to higher achievement   1   2   3   4   5

4. Utilizing game tactics and strategies   1   2   3   4   5

5. Applying conditioning principles   1   2   3   4   5

6. Teaching techniques during practice   1   2   3   4   5

7. Making coaching decisions during competitions   1   2   3   4   5

8. Conducting practice sessions   1   2   3   4   5

9. Planning for segments of yearly season   1   2   3   4   5

10. Developing game plans   1   2   3   4   5

Average: _____

Building the sport program:

11. Making recruiting contacts   1   2   3   4   5

12. Scouting opponents   1   2   3   4   5

13. Establishing a recruiting plan   1   2   3   4   5

14. Maintaining and using statistics   1   2   3   4   5

15. Recruiting a specific number of athletes   1 2 3 4 5

16. Recruiting quality athletes   1 2 3 4 5

Average: _____

Managing the sport program:

17. Monitoring athlete eligibility   1 2 3 4 5

18. Adhering to budget   1 2 3 4 5

19. Adhering to rules and regulations   1 2 3 4 5

20. Working relationships with department staff   1 2 3 4 5

21. Purchase of equipment   1 2 3 4 5

22. Being on time with paper work   1 2 3 4 5

23. Working relationships with peer coaches   1 2 3 4 5

24. Complying with institution's philosophy   1 2 3 4 5

Average: _____

Public relations:

25. Working with high school coaches   1 2 3 4 5

26. Conducting summer sports camps   1 2 3 4 5

27. Establishing working relationships with parents   1 2 3 4 5

28. Involvement with professional association   1 2 3 4 5

29. Presenting at player/coaching clinics   1 2 3 4 5

Average: _____

Team/athlete results:

30. Team win-loss record   1 2 3 4 5

31. Making the playoffs   1 2 3 4 5

32. Improvement from previous season   1 2 3 4 5

(continued)

(continued)

B.11 Committee Appraisal (Three-Year) Form: Coach Example

33. Improvement over current season   1   2   3   4   5

34. Performance of individual athlete(s)   1   2   3   4   5

Average: _____

Outcomes of coaching personal to the coach:

35. Receiving coaching awards   1   2   3   4   5

36. Writing for publication   1   2   3   4   5

37. Invited public appearances   1   2   3   4   5

38. Speaking engagements   1   2   3   4   5

39. Upgrading coach's certification   1   2   3   4   5

Average: _____

Overall average score: _____

Comments:

Potential for future success:

Overall assessment by athletic director:

Overall assessment by committee if different from that of athletic director:

Committee vote: _____ Yes   _____ No   _____ Abstentions

_____

Signature of Committee Chair

_____

Date

Solutions to the Case Studies

Appendix C contains notes and ideas for answering the case studies found at the end of each chapter. The case studies offered in each chapter posed a variety of different hypothetical problems that any manager could face, and the solutions presented here give valuable insight into the way a successful manager could handle these difficulties. By using these notes and ideas to help you answer the questions posed in the case studies, you can experience what it's like to be in the manager's shoes.

IN THE MANAGER'S SHOES

How in the World Do I Get Started? (pages 20-21)

David has already begun the process of developing a performance appraisal system because the first logical step in doing so is to assess the status quo. What methods, forms, rationale, and criteria are in current use? David's research has clarified that no procedure currently exists for his college or department. Knowing this, David must build a performance appraisal system specific to his situation, by using the following strategy:

1. Decide on purpose(s). David must be clear on what is expected of the evaluation system and why it is being used.

2. Gain the support of senior management and ensure that the development of a system incorporates college policy and procedure.

3. Because this is a small department, David will gather a committee-of-the-whole to communicate to everyone at once the need to develop a performance appraisal system. In this meeting, he should clarify why the system is needed, what it will be used for, and why. He should impress upon his colleagues the benefits of regular assessment for both the individual and the department. David needs to be open and encourage questions. He needs to outline a plan for how the procedure will be defined, along with his hope that everyone in the unit will play a part in helping to define it. A time line for meetings should be developed, and minutes of the discussion recorded. Sufficient time should be taken here to ensure reasonable levels of buy-in from department members.

4. In a larger department it might be recommended that a committee be appointed to focus the group on specific tasks. However, the department at St. Jessop's College is very small (11 people), and everything generated will need to be brand new. In such a case, the department might remain in the committee-of-the-whole formation. David, as athletic director, will be responsible for establishing common practices and possible options.

5. The group will begin by ensuring that all members share a common understanding of the unit's mission.

6. Next, the criteria for appraising each individual job will be defined. Each employee will play a prominent role in the

assessment of his or her job and the definition of job-specific performance criteria.

7. The procedure for performing the evaluation will be defined. Specifically, the questions *how, who, when,* and *how often* will be answered.

8. Once the criteria and method of evaluation are established, forms to aid in accomplishing the procedure will be designed.

9. Finally, the entire system of evaluation will be scrutinized and approved by the human resource experts within the organization.

Creating an Acceptance of Change (pages 21-22)

The following questions should be considered when conducting a paper work audit of current evaluation practices with managers:

- Are forms completed properly?
- Are the formal procedures of the system being followed?
- Are forms being used for the proper purpose?
- Is there evidence of thoughtful consideration and analysis in the written comments?
- Are individual assessments backed up by specific examples?
- Do you see trends in answers that might suggest overgeneralizing or central tendency?
- Do you believe that time is an issue? Are people taking too much time, or not giving enough?
- What employee comments result from the evaluation? Is there any pattern of comments?
- Is the appraisal procedure being followed in your department? Do employees have up-to-date information on file?

The following are some rating scale survey statements pertaining to the current evaluation system, which can be posed to managers and employees of the organization (7-point scale from "Totally disagree" to "Totally agree"):

- In our organization, there is agreement on what constitutes good performance.
- If you perform your job well, you will be recognized and rewarded.
- Employees who do not perform their job well will be confronted with the need to change.

- Most employees, line and staff, understand how the performance appraisal system works.
- Our evaluation system provides a good avenue for communication between superior and subordinate.
- In our organization, appraisals are done both fairly and precisely.
- The forms that we use to record assessments are complete and appropriate.
- It would not affect our business much if performance appraisals were not done.
- The department of human resources is very knowledgeable about performance appraisals and very effective in answering my questions.
- The outcomes of performance appraisal are important for the employees of our organization.

The Facilities Services Coordinator (pages 49-51)

1. Job assessment. The facilities services coordinator will be trained in the following areas: sport and sport facilities; sport rules; scheduling; event setup procedures; repairing equipment and troubleshooting; personnel supervision; personnel training; safety and risk management; dispute resolution; equipment dispensing, storage, and inventory; interface with customers; provisions for customer service; contribution to team-oriented working environment; paper work; punctuality; professionalism.

2. Job description. Responsibilities of this position include the following:
   a. Scheduling of facility
   b. Managing employees
   c. Setting up facility
   d. Managing equipment
   e. Providing customer service
   f. Overseeing risk management and ensuring safety
   g. Contributing to the organization's culture

3. Domain of performance
   a. Behavioral product factors: the number of safety audits performed yearly; the frequency of customer facility and set-up complaints; the quantity of equipment shrinkage on a yearly basis

      b. Behavioral process factors (task-related): effective scheduling of both facility and human resources; supervision and training of equipment staff; maintenance of a safe, clean, and welcoming building; management of an efficient and controlled equipment dispensing, retrieval, and storage area

      c. Behavioral process factors (maintenance-related): being on time with paper work; handling customer and employee complaints with diligence and attempting to solve problems quickly and effectively; contributing to a team-oriented work culture that is service-oriented and helpful at all times

4. Criteria types. A mixture of criteria types has been defined as per step #3 above.

5. Impact of the environment. The internal organizational environment, along with contextual factors of the external environment, must be assessed to ensure that the criteria are relevant and fair. An assessment of social, political, financial, and legal considerations and their impact on the job will enable the deletion of any criteria that fall outside the control of the job incumbent. In this case, with the criteria listed under step #3, the environment is not considered a threat to the integrity of these criteria.

Director of Marketing—Hawkley Golf & Country Club (pages 51-52)

Are the criteria for Michael's evaluation presented in the case study effective? Not really, because the criteria do not provide enough specific information about how Michael accomplishes his job. For instance, the first item on his job description relates to market research, forecasting, and planning. These factors are omitted from the evaluation criteria. The next difficulty relates to the fact that the number of new members and new sponsors attracted in a given year might represent effective overall performance, but these items might also be contaminated by factors of the environment. For instance, growth of the economy and an increase in disposable income might be important components of attracting new members and sponsors. The converse scenario, represented by tough economic times and correspondingly low membership and sponsorship, is also true. Therefore, measuring Michael's performance solely on the outcome of increased or decreased membership is dangerous because fluctuations may occur as a result of uncontrollable, external factors. It is just as important to investigate Michael's ability to professionally solicit, manage, and service sponsors as it is to observe the bottom line figures. The evaluation criteria presented in the case study say nothing of the development of promotional materials that will aid in the marketing efforts, nor is relationship-building mentioned.

The criteria listed by the board of directors are somewhat deficient as well. Criterion #1 relates to the bottom line financial viability of the club. Such a broad-based criterion will be affected by many factors outside of Michael's control, such as the management of the dining room, bar, and club concession areas; the pro shop; the course upkeep and management; the pricing of green fees; the attraction of special events; etc. The same argument that suggests the achievement on these criteria results from many sources within the organization is made for the board of directors' criterion #4 as well. The perception of board members about the overall image of the club cannot possibly be tied solely to the director of marketing. Image is a very broad construct, comes from all corners of the organization, and is influenced by everyone.

Finally, as this case is presented, it would be odd to have the board of directors receive the advice of the club professional regarding the marketing director's overall performance. They do not appear to work closely together, and there is no mention that Michael reports to the golf operations professional. Such input may be completely inappropriate.

The Barrington Bears Hockey Franchise and Coach Bill Boyd (page 79)

The Barrington Bears, and all of Barrington for that matter, have a solid understanding of the mission of the hockey franchise, as it is spelled out over the front entrance to the arena for all to see. As a first step, Peter believes that Bill is the best person to define the criteria for the performance management system and to ensure that the criteria are in step with the mission of the franchise. After all, no one could better know the intricacies of the job or the breadth of the tasks associated with completing it. Peter meets with Bill to outline this request and to set a time line for completion. He also communicates his part in accomplishing a performance management system—the time line and procedure to be used.

Taking the advice of his human resource buddy, Peter sets out to define an MBO performance appraisal system. In the development of his plan, he schedules goals meeting #1 in early June. He knows that the hockey competitive season will be completed in mid-April and that the fiscal year end of the organization is May 1. Scheduling the goals meeting for June will provide separation between the previous year and the upcoming one, but is not so far removed as to blur his recall of events.

At the goals meeting Peter and Bill will agree to the evaluation criteria and their priority weighting. The pair will also set specific goals for the upcoming year based on Bill's performance objectives, and set specific action plans to enable the accomplishment of the goals. A progress meeting will be held in December during the Christmas break as a check on Bill's progress toward goal achievement.

Next, Peter will collate performance data by collecting feedback from the athletes and parents about Bill's effectiveness as a coach. He decides to interview a half-dozen of the players' parents selected randomly each year and to collect survey data from the athletes. He also commits to watching parts of practices four or five times a month and to assessing Bill's coaching effectiveness during home games. Peter will also assess the content of Bill's operational planning of the franchise's home event management.

At the end of the year, the June meeting will serve to assess Bill's performance during the past season from the perspective of each of the criteria previously agreed to and the data collected and collated by Peter. Also at this meeting, goals for the coming year will be defined and action plans articulated. As is their custom, every other year all of this information will feed the contract renewal and renegotiation of salary processes.

A Performance Appraisal Interview Turned Nightmare (pages 79-80)

Brian was doomed from the beginning. First, he was late for the meeting. Then, he projected and verbalized impatience and a desire to move on to something more important. He immediately blurted out several of his perceptions of Michelle's ineffective performance without allowing her so much as a word, before even defining the purpose of the meeting. His cardinal sin, however, was basing his evaluation of her performance on his own (possibly largely unfounded) perceptions of Michelle's classes. She, on the other hand, although reacting rather strongly, had concrete evidence to back her class procedures and decisions regarding her classes. Basing an evaluation on an overheard conversation by two class participants is an enormous mistake. Brian needed to check the verifiable data that had been collected on the perceived effectiveness of Michelle's ability by her class participants. The same is true for his perception of her tardiness. His best course of action now is to apologize to Michelle and to seek another evaluation procedure for her through a different supervisor. If this is not possible, he will need to effectively start over again to try to rebuild a relationship for appraisal with Michelle through precise evaluation criteria and quantifiable assessments of effectiveness.

The introduction to the interview could have gone something like this:

> Brian: "Hi Michelle. Thanks for meeting with me. I really value the opportunity to sit and discuss your performance and involvement in the club this past year. With the frenetic pace around here we sometimes don't get the chance to talk often enough. Let me provide an overview of what I hope to accomplish in the next hour.
>
> "I'd like to start by talking about what you've been doing in your fitness classes and how you feel your class is responding to your approach. Then maybe we could discuss the overall atmosphere surrounding work for our instructors in the club. Finally, I'm interested in your future career plans and goals. I hope you will feel free to speak openly and honestly, as I assure you that our discussions will remain confidential.
>
> "Let's begin with your fitness classes. . . ."

The Hostile Appraisal Interview (pages 80-81)

Peter's mental checklist includes the following points:

- Be aware of body language: maintain eye contact, sit up to show attentiveness and interest.
- Stay calm and expect Brett to lose his cool.
- Keep voice even and don't interrupt Brett; let him talk and listen to his side.
- Questions are better than statements that can be taken offensively.
- Try not to lay blame and keep the focus of the interview on Brett.
- Ensure that we deal with any problems discussed, or at a minimum define how we intend to deal with them and when.
- Be prepared to disagree on events that might be perceived to have happened, but don't lose focus on defining what needs to be done in the future to alleviate performance concerns.
- Ensure that we leave the interview with a specific course of action.
- Find the positive as well as the negative.

Winning and the Performance of School Coaches (pages 94-95)

It is always better to have several indices of effectiveness as opposed to only one or two. And in the case of outcome factors, it is clearly substantiated by appraisal research that too much emphasis on outcome factors as the prime arbiter of successful performance is very dangerous. An overemphasis on outcome factors tends to result in an organizational culture in which individuals become extremely self-centered in their approach to the job. A "me and mine" culture prevails and competition for resources and the pursuit of one's own goals are emphasized over all other values. Never mind the goals of the organization or the need for a team-oriented approach to achievement!

"Winning" as the primary criteria of successful athletic coaching is further complicated by the very nature of sport. For every winner there will be a loser. The best performance, the best strategy and preparation, might not align with the winning team. A coach whose team loses the contest might have done an extremely effective job because a multitude of factors contribute to coaching effectiveness and winning.

The argument provided above is true no matter the scenario or level of sport. Coaching is multidimensional regardless of age group or setting. However, the importance of winning to the organization and its ability to achieve its mission based on the importance of winning within that mission might vary depending on the sport setting. It is conceivable that winning will be of higher importance to a professional sport franchise in which entertainment value and business objectives through profit margins take on greater importance. The entire appraisal package and objectives must mesh with the mission of the organization, and winning within the sport context is an important component requiring clarity beginning with the mission of the organization.

Evaluating Volunteer Staff (pages 95-96)

Karen's committee needs to develop some policy for the soccer league. In order to specifically deal with the issue of overextension as seen with coach Doug, the league might choose to implement a rule encouraging coaches to lead only one team within certain age groups that can be scheduled to avoid conflicts. The guidelines for coaches might also include other philosophical principles to help ensure that all the volunteers coaching in the league operate similarly with respect to playing time, inculcating principles like fair play and respect for officials, and the amount of time being required for practices. These guidelines can then help the league formulate the basis of evaluation through common principles of operation for all volunteer coaches. Has the volunteer met his responsibility for managing the team? Has Doug organized the practices and games; ensured that equipment is present; made sure that every boy and girl got approximately equal playing time; ensured that, win or lose, everyone shakes hands and receives positive reinforcement about things done well; made sure that all participants have ultimately had some fun? These guiding principles then help provide a basis on which to evaluate the performance of the volunteer coach. Karen's committee can discuss each of these factors in an unthreatening, fairly informal year-end meeting with the coaches. Doug could be advised that he is doing a terrific job but that coaching more than one team within the age groups he is currently committed to creates too many scheduling overlaps. He could be encouraged to shift his commitment or to get a couple of others to help him out as assistant coaches and lead the team when he has a conflict. In this way, Doug is unlikely to become alienated and walk away from the coaching because of criticism he perceives as unfair. In addition, some control of the operating principles of the league is maintained without a rigorous evaluation of an individual who is volunteering his time and who is likely to perceive a formal evaluation of his contribution as unfair.

A Further Look at Hawkley Golf & Country Club (pages 113-114)

1. Regular interaction with actual members of the board.

2. An opportunity for regular discussions and the interchange of ideas and feedback on both marketing initiatives and the "Hawkley image."

3. Guidance for Arnie with respect to goals, and the motivation to be both goal- and achievement-oriented.

4. A means of communicating the board of directors' support and awareness of his hard work to ensure that Arnie is conscious of the degree to which the club championed and appreciated his efforts.

5. A better way of linking Arnie's contribution to the organization with his compensation package, instead of creating an environment of token rewards. Tokens of appreciation for outstanding work are often welcomed in the early years, but they quickly become tiresome and seem downright condescending after 16 years.

Arnie left his job because he felt unappreciated. He is aware of his value to the organization but feels that the board of directors is uninterested in him. It would be appropriate for Hawkley to form a three-person committee of the board to guide the marketing initiatives of the organization, thereby providing interest and feedback in what is surely an important facet of club operations. Another three-person personnel committee should perform the communication and goal-setting function with Arnie through MBO.

Cynthia Carrington and Hawkley Golf & Country Club (pages 114-115)

1. No reporting structure or supervisor
2. No communication regarding priority status within the job description
3. Assessment of performance based on criteria other than those agreed to at the beginning of the job
4. Dismissal related to the development of a marketing plan and philosophy that corresponds to proper marketing theory (short-term pain for long-term gain)
5. No mention of specific time lines for realizing goals
6. Dismissal communicated in terms that are somewhat unrelated to the job, not to mention illegal: "not quite the 'type of person' they needed at this time."

Organizational structure provides the job incumbent with a chain of command to enable feedback on smaller, ongoing decisions instead of a "sink or swim" mentality. A system of communication, in addition to a structure for decision making, are both critical elements of the definition of job expectations. The law reinforces that specific performance standards must be communicated to employees, and that appraisal must be conducted within a standardized, formalized system. In addition, an appeal system needs to be made available to the employee who disagrees with the assessment.

And Then There Was "Super Dave" (pages 115-116)

An MBO system of evaluation may very well have prevented or lessened the scandal that rocked Hawkley. This particular appraisal system would involve early meetings to determine the ways and means to accomplish goals. With such supervision, it is quite possible that Super Dave's fraud would have been identified before his implementation of his "give it away" marketing philosophy. With the appraisal system in place, at the very least, attention to Dave's activities would have been heightened and the organization would have been more apt to operate with procedures that constituted a checks-and-balances system in its operations and management.

REFERENCES

Barber, H., & Eckrich, J. (1998). Methods and criteria employed in the evaluation of intercollegiate coaches. *Journal of Sport Management, 12,* 301-322.

Bernardin, H.J., Alvarez, K.M., & Cranny, C.J. (1976). A re-comparison of behavioral expectation scales to summated scales. *Journal of Applied Psychology, 61,* 564-570.

Birrell, S.J. (1989). Racial relations theories and sport: Hot and cool. *International Review of Sport Sociology, 6,* 212-227.

Blum, M.L., & Naylor, J.C. (1968). *Industrial psychology.* New York: Harper & Row.

Brief, A.P. (1998). *Attitudes in and around organizations.* Thousand Oaks, CA: Sage.

Buford, J.A., Burkhalter, B.B., & Jacobs, G.T. (1988). Link job descriptions to performance appraisal. *Personnel Journal, 6,* 132-140.

Byars, L.L., & Rue, L.W. (1979). *Personnel management: Concepts and application.* Philadelphia: W.B. Saunders.

Camy, J. (1996). Sport management in France. In J.-L. Chappelet & M.-H. Roukhadze (Eds.), *Sport management: An international approach.* Lausanne: International Olympic Committee.

Carroll, S.J., & Schneier, C.E. (1982). *Performance appraisal and review systems.* Glenview, IL: Scott Foresman.

Chelladurai, P. (1999). *Human resource management in sport and recreation.* Champaign, IL: Human Kinetics.

Cline, T.R., & Wilmoth, G.H. (1987). *Superior-subordinate communication, coorientation, and satisfaction.* Paper presented at the annual meeting of the International Communication Association, Montreal.

Coakley, J.J. (1986). *Sport in society. Issues and controversies.* St. Louis: Mosby.

Deets, N.R., & Tyler, D.T. (1986). How Xerox improved its performance appraisals. *Personnel Journal, 4,* 50-52.

Dolan, S.L., & Schuler, R.S. (1987). *Personnel and human resource management in Canada.* New York: West.

Drucker, P.F. (1954). *The practice of management.* New York: Harper & Row.

Fleishman, E.A., & Mumford, M.D. (1991). Evaluating classifications of job behavior: A construct validation of the Ability Requirement Scales. *Personnel Psychology: A Journal of Applied Research, 3,* 523-576.

Goldstein, J.H. (1979). *Sports, games and play. Social and psychological viewpoints.* Hillsdale, NJ: Erlbaum.

Grote, R.C. (1996). *The complete guide to performance appraisal.* New York: American Management Association.

Hall, A., Slack, T., Smith, G., & Whitson, D. (1991). *Sport in Canadian society.* Toronto: McClelland and Stewart.

Horn, T.S. (1985). Coaches' feedback and changes in children's perceptions of physical competence. *Journal of Educational Psychology, 77,* 174-186.

Horn, T.S. (1992). *Advances in sport psychology.* Champaign, IL: Human Kinetics.

Ilgen, D.R., & Barnes-Farrell, J.L. (1984). Performance planning and evaluation. In J.E. Rosenzweig & F.E. Kast (Eds.), *Modules in management.* Chicago: Science Research Associates.

Ivancevich, J.M., & Glueck, W.G. (1989). *Foundations of personnel: Human resource management.* Boston: BPI/Irwin.

James, L. (1973). Criterion models and construct validity for criteria. *Psychological Bulletin, 80,* 75-83.

Jobling, I., & Deane, J. (1996). Sport management in Australia: A socio-historical overview and tertiary education perspective. In J.-L. Chappelet & M.-H. Roukhadze (Eds.), *Sport management: An international approach.* Lausanne: International Olympic Committee.

Kane, J.S., Bernardin, H.J., Villanova, P., & Peyrefitte, J. (1995). Stability of rater leniency: Three studies. *Academy of Management Journal, 4,* 1036-1051.

Landy, F.J., & Farr, J.L. (1980). Performance rating. *Psychological Bulletin, 87,* 72-107.

Landy, F.J., & Farr, J.L. (1982). *Performance rating. The Performance Appraisal Sourcebook.* Amherst, MA: Human Resources Development.

Landy, F.J., & Farr, J.L. (1983). *The measurement of work performance: Methods, theory and application.* New York: Academic Press.

Latham, G.P., & Wexley, K.N. (1981). *Increasing productivity through performance appraisal.* Reading, MA: Addison-Wesley.

Levy, M. (1989). Almost-perfect performance appraisals. *Personnel Journal, 4,* 76-83.

Locke, E.A., & Latham, G.P. (1984). *Goal setting: A motivational technique that works.* Englewood Cliffs, NJ: Prentice-Hall.

Locke, E.A., & Latham, G.P. (1990). *A theory of goal setting and task performance.* Englewood Cliffs, NJ: Prentice-Hall.

MacLean, J.C. (1992). *Coaching evaluation criteria: Assessing the integrity of a theoretical model for sport administrators in Canadian universities.* Unpublished doctoral dissertation, The Ohio State University, Columbus.

MacLean, J.C. (1993). Coaching evaluation: A guide for establishing job-specific criteria. *Applied Research in Coaching and Athletics Annual,* 44-60.

MacLean, J.C. (1997). *An investigation into the measurability of performance appraisal criteria.* Paper presented at the annual conference of the North American Society for Sport Management, May 28-30. San Antonio, TX.

MacLean, J.C. (1998). *Performance appraisal criteria: A retrospective look at training and evaluation in sport management.* Paper presented at the annual conference of the North American Society for Sport Management, May 28-30. Buffalo, NY.

MacLean, J.C., & Chelladurai, P. (1995). Dimensions of coaching performance: Development of a scale. *Journal of Sport Management, 2,* 194-207.

MacLean, J.C., & Zakrajsek, D. (1994). Evaluating athletic coaches: A descriptive analysis of Canadian universities. *Canadian Association for Health, Physical Education, & Recreation Journal, 2,* 5-10.

MacLean, J.C., & Zakrajsek, D. (1996). Factors considered important for evaluating Canadian university athletic coaches. *Journal of Sport Management, 4,* 446-462.

Maier, N.R.F. (1958). Three types of appraisal interviews. *Personnel, 34,* 27-29.

McKenna, E., & Beech, N. (1995). *The essence of human resource management.* Englewood Cliffs, NJ: Prentice-Hall.

McKirchy, K. (1998). *Powerful performance appraisals.* Franklin Lakes, NJ: Career Press.

Montgomery, J., & Fewer, W. (1988). *Family systems and beyond.* New York: Human Sciences.

Murphy, K.R., & Cleveland, J.N. (1991). *Performance appraisal: An organizational perspective.* Boston: Allyn and Bacon.

Nixon, H.L., & Frey, J.H. (1996). *A sociology of sport.* New York: Wadsworth.

O'Reilly, C.A., III, & Anderson, J.C. (1980). Trust and the communication of performance appraisal information: The effect of feedback on performance and job satisfaction. *Human Communication Research, 6,* 290-298.

Orlick, T. (1980). *In pursuit of excellence.* Ottawa: Coaching Association of Canada.

Raia, A.P. (1974). *Managing by objectives.* Glencoe, IL: Scott Foresman.

Redding, W.C. (1972). *Communication within the organization: An interpretive review of theory and research.* New York: Industrial Communication Council.

Saal, F.E., & Knight, P.A. (1995). *Industrial/organizational psychology: Science and practice* (2nd ed.). Pacific Grove, CA: Brooks/Cole.

Sashkin, M. (1981). *Assessing performance appraisal.* San Diego: University Associates.

Schuler, R.S., & Jackson, S.E. (1996). *Human resource management: Positioning for the 21st century* (6th ed.). Minneapolis: West.

Shilbury, D. (1996). Towards Sydney 2000: Precipitating sport management planning in Australia. In J.-L. Chappelet & M.-H. Roukhadze (Eds.), *Sport management: An international approach.* Lausanne: International Olympic Committee.

Smilansky, J. (1997). *The new hr.* Boston: International Thomson Business Press.

Smith, P.C. (1976). Behaviors, results and organizational effectiveness. In M. Dunnette (Ed.), *Handbook of industrial and organizational psychology.* Chicago: Rand-McNally.

Smith, P.C., & Kendall, L.M. (1963). Retranslation of expectations: An approach to the construction of unambiguous anchors for rating scales. *Journal of Applied Psychology, 47,* 149-155.

Sport Canada: Human Resource Management and National Team Coaches. (1987). *Fitness & amateur sport.* Ottawa: Government of Canada.

Stone, T.H., & Meltz, N.M. (1988). *Human resource management in Canada.* Toronto: Holt, Rinehart and Winston of Canada, Ltd.

Swan, W.S. (1991). *How to do a superior performance appraisal.* New York: John Wiley & Sons.

Tompkins, N.C. (1997). *Managing employee performance problems.* Menlo Park, CA: Crisp.

Tornow, W.W., & London, M. (1998). *Maximizing the value of 360-degree feedback. A process for successful individual and organizational development.* San Francisco: Jossey-Bass.

Wheeless, L.R., Wheeless, V.E., & Howard, R.D. (1984). The relationships of communication with supervisor and decision participation to employee job satisfaction. *Communication Quarterly, 32,* 222-232.

Williams, R.S. (1998). *Performance management. Perspectives on employee performance.* Boston: International Thomson Business Press.

Wriston, W.B. (1992). The state of American management. In W. Bennis (Ed.), *Leaders on leadership. Interviews with top executives* (pp. 3-12). Boston: Harvard Business Review.

INDEX

ABOUT THE AUTHOR

Joanne MacLean, PhD, has been on the faculty at the University of Windsor in Ontario, Canada, since 1985. Currently, she is an associate professor in sport management on the faculty of human kinetics.

Dr. MacLean completed graduate studies in both Canada and the United States at the University of New Brunswick and The Ohio State University. She has managed collegiate sport programs and actively studied personnel management. Dr. MacLean also has extensive experience coaching basketball at both the high school and collegiate levels, including coaching the Canadian junior national team. She has numerous awards and honors recognizing her basketball playing and coaching career. These honors include two Athlete of the Year awards and five Coach of the Year awards at the high school and university levels.

Dr. MacLean chairs the Canadian Women's National Basketball Program Operations Committee and is a member of the Canadian Basketball Program's Elite Performance Committee for Canada Basketball. She is an executive member of Ontario University Athletics and chairs the department of athletics & recreational services at the University of Windsor.